Praise for *Saltwater Mansions*

'*Saltwater Mansions* delves into an engrossing mystery through a kaleidoscope of lives, and the result is thrilling, moving and searingly profound. I loved it'
  Chris Whitaker, author of *All the Colours of the Dark*

'I inhaled it in a sitting – what an exhilarating book. Brave, revealing and unexpected, this is a wise and original exploration of the extraordinary nature of ordinary lives and how they are interpreted by others'
  Cathy Rentzenbrink, author of *The Last Act of Love*

'Brilliant. A proper read-it-in-one-go book, opening up an advent calendar of lives behind the doors of a block of flats. Beautifully written, humane and soul-baring'
  Adam Kay, author of *This Is Going to Hurt*

'Magnificently told and devastatingly moving, *Saltwater Mansions* is a treasure trove of human truths – a bittersweet dive into the profundity, melancholy and strange sweetness of being alive, bound by a totally original, utterly compelling true crime narrative'
  Harriet Gibsone, author of *Is This OK?*

'An utterly incredible book. The memoir of a seaside town, a portrait of an absence, and a hymn of grief. I am still thinking about it'
  Dan Davies, author of *In Plain Sight: The Life and Lies of Jimmy Savile*

'A beautiful, humane, compelling book. What begins as a humble inquiry into a small-town missing person's case becomes a plaintive, intricately nested set of untold stories. Each quietly extraordinary person who's entangled in this narrative is illuminated with such vividness and compassion you can't help but recognise the fragments of your own experience in all of them. David Whitehouse has always been a brilliant writer of Britain's overlooked characters, and this is his finest work yet'
Benjamin Wood, author of *The Young Accomplice*

'David Whitehouse is such an original and compassionate writer. His search for the mysterious Caroline Lane is engrossing and intriguing . . . a remarkable book'
Donald McRae, author of *The Last Bell*

'Compelling, insightful, moving. I don't know where to start with describing how much I loved this book'
Jennie Godfrey, author of *The List of Suspicious Things*

'No other writer could go out for a haircut and wind up years later with a treatise on why we ask *why?* that reads like a diary, a thriller, a tribute to all the world's untold stories and the lost art and tragedies of being unknown'
Michael Holden, author of *The Reluctant Carer*

'A gripping mystery that becomes an immersive journey into memory, legacy and grief. *Saltwater Mansions* is a story masterfully told by David Whitehouse, and it will stay with you long after you reach the end'
Neil Forsyth, writer and creator of *The Gold*

Saltwater Mansions

David Whitehouse is the author of three acclaimed novels. His first, *Bed*, won the 2012 Betty Trask Prize. His second, *Mobile Library*, won the 2015 Jerwood Fiction Prize. In 2022, his debut non-fiction book, *About A Son*, was shortlisted for the Gordon Burn Prize and the CWA Gold Dagger for Non-Fiction. His journalism has appeared in the *Guardian*, *Esquire*, *The Times* and many other publications, and he has also written extensively for the screen. He lives in Margate.

Also by David Whitehouse

About A Son
Bed
Mobile Library
The Long Forgotten

Saltwater Mansions

The woman who disappeared
and other untold stories

David Whitehouse

PHOENIX

First published in Great Britain in 2025 by Phoenix Books,
an imprint of The Orion Publishing Group Ltd
Carmelite House, 50 Victoria Embankment
London EC4Y 0DZ

An Hachette UK Company

The authorised representative in the EEA is Hachette Ireland,
8 Castlecourt Centre, Dublin 15, D15 XTP3, Ireland (email: info@hbgi.ie)

1 3 5 7 9 10 8 6 4 2

Copyright © Slow Down Ltd 2025

The moral right of David Whitehouse to be identified as
the author of this work has been asserted in accordance
with the Copyright, Designs and Patents Act of 1988.

All rights reserved. No part of this publication may be
reproduced, stored in a retrieval system, or transmitted
in any form or by any means, electronic, mechanical,
photocopying, recording, or otherwise, without the
prior permission of both the copyright owner and the
above publisher of this book.

A CIP catalogue record for this book is
available from the British Library.

ISBN (Hardback) 978 1 3996 2197 7
ISBN (Ebook) 978 1 3996 2200 4
ISBN (Audio) 978 1 3996 2201 1

Typeset by Input Data Services Ltd, Bridgwater, Somerset

Printed in Great Britain by Clays Ltd, Elcograf, S.p.A.

MIX
Paper | Supporting
responsible forestry
FSC® C104740

www.orionbooks.co.uk
www.phoenix-books.co.uk

For Elmer

The story you are about to read is a work of non-fiction. Some names and details have been changed to protect the identities of those concerned. Where the author wasn't present, occasional scenes have been dramatised for narrative purposes. The intention, though, is to keep the truth intact.

One

As I walked along Margate promenade, the beach was full from berm to shore. Pinkening idlers bobbed in shallow water. Eager children dug in hot sand. Teens on beers threw themselves off the harbour arm under a heatwave sun the orange of blood in yolk. The view, if they ever looked back, was of a town in constant flux, and the scars left behind by violent changes in fortune: deprivation and regeneration, exodus and influx, faded glamour and fresh wind. I knew nothing yet of the woman who had vanished, but this was the perfect place to disappear, if that was what you needed, or were made, to do.

    Peeling off at the clock tower, I cut towards the High Street, a hill from the job centre to the sea. Halfway up it stands the entrance to a small shopping precinct called The Centre, where my friend, Grace, had just opened a hair salon. I'd hidden my surprise when she first told me about it. I know nothing about business and even less about hairdressing, still, opening a hair salon off the High Street didn't make a whole lot of sense. Margate is a tourist town. The cafes, art galleries and souvenir shops that draw day trippers and their money from the beach are clustered around the quaint cobbled roads of the Old Town, down at the bottom by the coast.

The High Street has little of that same seaside charm. It comprises a squat strip of pound stores, bookmakers and fast-food restaurants, pocked by the wounds of empty units that closed for good when their customers were lured to the giant out-of-town shopping centre at Westwood Cross. Visitors don't travel this far from the front, so these streets are left to the sedate pace and shallow pockets of the locals. The Centre seems a tough place to make a new salon, a new anything, much of a success.

But Margate has been changing lately. Suddenly a bunch of new businesses have opened in The Centre that feel more like the kind you might find in gentrified Portland, Hackney or Brooklyn than in a run-down, faded English coastal town for so long synonymous with unemployment, shut pubs and bored youth. Now there's Mariachi, a mezcal and tequila bar. Curve, the flagship store of a Margate-based speciality coffee roasters. Elsewhere sells craft beers and second-hand records above an intimate basement music venue. And across the courtyard, Palms Pizzeria does a fennel sausage, nduja and red onion pizza as wide as a tyre.

Grace had always wanted a place, a chair, a mirror of her own. Though the vacant unit in The Centre was small and hidden away in a corner, she knew it would be perfect for her needs. She plumbed in a sink, painted the walls bubblegum pink and peppered them with pages torn from glossy 1990s fashion magazines, *Playboy* and posters of Pamela Anderson. When it was done, she named the salon 'Rinsed', its logo designed with colourful dots between the letters, like the titles from the sitcom *Friends*. On the morning she opened for business she finally left behind the long, difficult days of doing cuts at home while her two young daughters blasted one another with the dryer. In the five years since she arrived in Margate, the town, like her dreams, had come alive.

While Grace cut my hair we made small talk about how hot it was outside. We have children of the same age who attend the same school, so we compared notes on their teachers, and how tough it is raising kids. I'd moved here from London too, in 2015, when my partner Lou was pregnant with the first of our two sons and the realities of renting a small flat in the city with a baby quickly revealed themselves to be deranged.

Grace wanted to know about my latest book, so we spoke for a while about that, and she asked what I was working on next. The truth was nothing, but I didn't feel able to get into the reasons why, so instead I said I didn't really know.

There was a pause then, a brief moment of silence that at the time felt natural, but which, on reflection, Grace might have manufactured, as if to bring my focus to what she was about to say, this thing that I might need to hear.

'I've got a story for you,' she said. It was something her previous client, Dee, whose hair Grace dyed pale pink, had told her just an hour or so before. 'I haven't been able to stop thinking about it since. I'll tell you. But if I do, you won't be able to stop thinking about it either.' The scissors were still and her eyes were vivid. This was her guarantee.

It was a year or so ago when Dee moved into a top-floor flat at Saltwater Mansions further along the esplanade. There was no lift and lots of stairs, up which she had to lug what seemed like a hundred boxes or more. She'd barely even begun to unpack when she discovered something had happened there, something remarkable, to the woman who lived on the ground floor. A woman named Caroline Lane.

Caroline Lane moved into flat nine, Saltwater Mansions, almost two decades ago, in the summer of 2005. There wasn't anything particularly unusual about Caroline. Those who met her might have said she kept herself to herself, but there was nothing peculiar about that. They'd all have said she was intelligent, stylish and well dressed. What conversations they'd had with her hinted at a good job and sophisticated interests. She enjoyed going to the theatre. She liked literature and art galleries, that kind of thing. She didn't miss a mortgage payment. She always paid her council tax and TV licence on time. There were never any problems with noise or parties, like there was in some of the other flats. She didn't have a dog that would shit all over the car park. And she never left the building's communal front door open at night. On paper, she was a perfect neighbour. The problem was that these days she only existed on paper. If there was anything strange about Caroline Lane, it was that Caroline Lane wasn't there.

The last time anyone in Saltwater Mansions saw Caroline was in May 2009. Since then the neighbours had tried to find her lots of times, but it never came to anything. Even the private detectives they hired drew blanks. Nobody could give any reasonable explanation for her absence. Nor for how a series of automated bank transfers maintained a life she didn't appear to be living. Perhaps stranger still was that no one ever came looking for her. No one called asking where she was and no one reported her missing. In fact, there wasn't a single other person whose life seemed to change in any way at all when 45-year-old Caroline Lane vanished from the centre of her own.

Dee hadn't been living in Saltwater Mansions long, but she and a few of the neighbours quickly became friends. It was that kind of building. People chatted on the stairs and caught up by the bins. They looked out for one another when and how they could. Some of them would meet in flat five every couple of months for a glass of wine. These nights would always end the same way; it was never long before they were talking about Caroline. Trading theories about what might have happened to her had become a grimly irresistible collective pastime. Did she take her own life? Was she abducted? Was she killed? Did she have a breakdown? Was she who she said she was at all? Then, by the end of the first bottle, the questions would deepen. Why did nobody notice? How does someone just disappear off the face of the earth like that? And what does it say about the world we live in if they do? They were questions without answers. They were stories without ends.

For the residents of Saltwater Mansions, thirteen years of absence made Caroline the subject of a shared obsession. How could it not? It was wild and strange, big and unsettling, and they were reminded of it every time they passed her door. She had vanished, yet she was still there. The heart of a mystery. The ghost in a ghost story. The missing woman of flat nine, Saltwater Mansions, Caroline Lane.

Grace was right. I couldn't stop thinking about it. The mystery of Caroline Lane was as alluring as it was sad. As Dee had explained it when she'd sat in this chair: the search had been all but abandoned. The trail had gone cold. Nobody even turned up asking where Caroline was. If it wasn't for the handful of Saltwater Mansions residents obsessed by her fate – if it wasn't for Dee telling Grace about her one day at the hairdressers – she might have been forgotten entirely.

There were groups of friends and smiling families outside the salon, laughing and enjoying the sunshine together. So perhaps it was the weather, perhaps it was my mood, or perhaps it was a combination of both, but by the time Grace finished cutting my hair, I'd decided that, when I left the salon, I was going to go straight to Saltwater Mansions to try and find out about Caroline for myself. It was a decision that would have a profound impact on me and those I love, one that would come to dominate the next year of my life.

When I think about this moment, I remember one of my favourite lines from *The Simpsons*, when Chief Wiggum catches his son Ralph and Bart trying to get into a locked cupboard in his attic: 'What is your fascination with my forbidden closet of mystery?' But if I was to tell you that mere curiosity is what drove me up the esplanade that day, it would be a lie. Curiosity – strong, persistent, writerly or otherwise – is only a part of why I fell down the rabbit hole of Caroline Lane.

I can now see the real reason clearly, but that too would be disingenuous to include here, because I didn't really know – or was unable to acknowledge – it at the time. I can only say that the truth was obscured from me by the intense opacity of something I could barely comprehend. Looking back, I understand it better. Now I see that Caroline's story was not the only one I was searching for. But sometimes you have to get to the end to see what brought you to the start.

I waved goodbye to Grace through the salon window and headed for Saltwater Mansions. Into the sun, along the front and past the beach, where once I disappeared too.

Two

My parents had three kids by August 1986, so they were experienced enough to know that, between the sunburn and the tantrums and the chances of drowning, a trip to the seaside with children was about as taxing a family day out as it was possible to endure. On the train that morning they made their case for Broadstairs, a couple of miles round the Thanet coast. There were fewer tourists there. It was unfussy and posh, quaint and serene. Refining their sales pitch as we neared the station, they swore the sand was better too. Finer. More golden. A dream for building castles. But their children, Alison, Glenn and I, lobbied hard for Margate; its famous fairground and snaggle-toothed front of amusement arcades, loud and colourful and working as designed, to suck us from the beach and the change from their pockets.

A trip to the seaside was a rare thing for our family. Money was an issue. Not yet perilously, but there wasn't enough of it. And home was Nuneaton, in the middle of the Midlands, about as far from the ocean as it was possible in Britain to get. This was to be the highlight of the few days we were to spend visiting Mum's side of the family in Chatham, a Medway town about an hour up the track. That's where Mum and Dad first met, at Chatham Dockyard, in October 1968.

Keith Whitehouse was in the Royal Navy, an electrician who slept in the belly of a warship. Gill Vizard was sixteen and pretty, her hair coaxed into a neat little beehive. She lived round the corner on Silver Hill, where a trembling suitor once posted a love letter through her door with a poem that began 'Jill, Jill from Silver Hill . . .' (she spelt her name Gill because it was short for Gillian, but everyone else spelt it Jill, so there was some confusion later, among her children, over whether she'd gone through life spelling her own name wrong). The boy was nice enough but she didn't fancy him. She could only think about Keith. His short scruff of curly black hair. How handsome he looked in his uniform.

Within a couple of months, Keith had her name – with a G – tattooed on his forearm, scrawled across a heart between the words 'true' and 'love', above a bluish seabird already beginning to blur. She was angry and embarrassed but secretly enamoured. His smile got it past her father.

The five of us stepped out of the station and the sight of the main sands unfurled as a scene from a pilgrimage, a mass of people stretching to the lip of an ocean withdrawn as though ceding the land. It seemed inconceivable there might be space for us. I clung to Mum's hand even more tightly than usual. I'd a fear of getting lost that some mistook for shyness. I wasn't shy. I just enjoyed listening to the conversations of adults. I liked hearing the stories they told one another and the things they revealed about themselves. But I was also convinced that if I was to stray from my mother's line of sight I'd never see her again. So I was always at her ankles in one way or another, my knuckles bunched in the hem of her dress.

Dad lifted our bags from the pavement. He was a strong man with broad shoulders and a determined sheen to his eyes.

In some small but never-closing drawer of my imagination he was made from rocks (the shape of him, those big arms, wide fists, a boulderish back and chest; I'd once watched him pick up a fridge). He would approach the task ahead – to lay our towel down on the sand, to set up camp – with the same unimpeachable momentum with which he approached everything he did. To keep moving forwards until the job was done. He prided himself on that. I was too young but somehow understood it anyway: never looking back was his thing. We followed him along the promenade through the thickening crowd.

Mum remembered Margate from her own childhood. She came when she was seven with her parents and four siblings on a day trip in August 1958. They were armed with sandwiches and flasks of tea because they couldn't afford to eat in the bustling cafes at the base of the harbour arm, where the women wore elegant dresses and the men wool suits despite the heat.

Their family had been the first on Silver Hill to get a TV, for the Queen's coronation in 1952, so they already knew who the famous comedian Eric Morecambe was when their father, Bill, told them Morecambe had married Miss Margate, Joan Bartlett, and that they'd had their wedding reception above The Bull's Head, the busy pub run by Bartlett's father in the Old Town, which stood before them now. Mum sat outside it eating an ice cream, and as she licked the drips that streaked like missiles down the cone she thought the whole place impossibly glamorous. More how she imagined the Mediterranean than the drizzly, attritional Britain she knew.

Dad remembered Margate too. His family holidayed here when he was a child. There were six of them, all sharing a small room in a little guest house, net curtains stained with rococo curls of yellow by decades of cigarette smoke: him, his parents, two brothers and a sister, Ann. He was the youngest. The room was cramped, only fit for sleeping or arguing, so they'd hit the beach at sunrise and not return before nightfall. Their parents would rent candy-striped deckchairs and keep their shoes on. The kids would go paddling and digging, begging change for another ride on a forlorn donkey, or to pay the man who'd let them have a photograph with his pet monkey. They'd chosen that week because it was the factory worker's holiday and Dad's father, my granddad Douglas, had time off. It meant nothing much then, but years later this small, crucial detail allowed my parents to say they'd been on the same beach on the same day when they were children. Maybe even close enough to touch.

They both recalled fizzing with excitement as they approached the west end of the promenade. This was the entrance to Dreamland, an amusement park that, beside the sands, had long been the town's biggest draw. It had a big wheel and an ornate carousel, but its main attraction was the Scenic Railway, the oldest rollercoaster in the UK, distinctive for being made entirely from an elegant lattice of wood and requiring a brakeman to travel with the train, manually controlling its speed. A strong wind carried the screams of the passengers as far as it carried the gulls.

By the time I first visited Margate in the summer of 1986, the Scenic Railway's rickety charm stood in stark contrast to the Looping Star, an ugly steel rollercoaster the Dutch Bembom brothers had introduced when they bought the park in 1981 and changed its name to Bembom Brothers White Knuckle Theme Park. While the new name left punters in no doubt what they were paying for, it lumbered uglily on the tongue. But like most British seaside business owners, the Bembom brothers were stuck somewhere between the old and the new, wrestling with how best to combat a looming threat to their very existence.

Margate's traditional economic base, the one my parents had been a part of – working-class holidaymakers staying for a week or more, supplemented by day trippers on weekends and public holidays – had started to crumble. The rise of cheap package holidays abroad in the early 1980s sounded a death knell for residential holiday trade, effectively destroying footfall on summer weekdays. While weekends remained buoyant, the shift obliterated five-sevenths of the seaside economy. This loss of revenue meant the town struggled to maintain its infrastructure, which in turn began to erode its appeal. At five years old, I only took in the big wheel's size, not the rust round its rivets. But by 1986 Margate was showing signs of weariness. The slow, undeniable beginnings of a corrosive, catastrophic decline.

We eventually found a spot on the beach. Mum unrolled the windbreak. Dad thumped it into the sand with a mallet. I was exhilarated by the sweet-salt tang of brine and candyfloss air, the noise of hundreds of children playing in the blinding white sunlight that flashed off the water. I forgot about getting lost and followed my brother and sister to the edge of the ocean. I liked watching the surf swallow my feet, the dizzying feeling as the earth slid back and forth beneath me. I inched forwards, hopping the waves, up to my ankles, then my knees, then my hips. I enjoyed pretending one of them might knock me over, right up until one of them did.

The tide pulled me out until the water was deeper than I was tall and held me underneath it. I tried to right myself, but could no more feel anything beneath me than I could rise upwards to where I needed to be. Had I a fatal misunderstanding of how land works? Was it not that the ground gently tapered beneath the ocean, down to the bed? Was the edge of a country in fact a ledge? And if you fell from it, was your destiny as mine seemed now: to be forever tumbling, foul cold saltwater flooding my throat, the remorseless blackening sea.

Maybe seconds passed slowly, maybe minutes fast, before the tide pushed me in face down and head first. My eyes and mouth were bunged with wet sand. I scooped it out so that I could see, so that I could breathe, and found myself in a new place entirely. None of the landmarks – the big wheel, the Bembom Brothers' sign, the slimy green rock of the tidal pool's walls – were where they'd been when I entered the water. The sea had dragged me down the shoreline. My world had been hastily redrawn.

I wandered for a while until a woman heard me crying. She used her towel to wipe my eyes and asked me if I knew where my parents were. I couldn't catch my breath to tell her they were gone.

It was some time before my dad emerged from the crowd. He called my name. We thought you'd disappeared, he said, and he carried me back in his arms.

Three

What should have been a twenty-minute walk from Grace's salon to Saltwater Mansions took longer in the heat. I found it down a backstreet, far enough from the main sands that the noise of arcades dimmed to nothing. This was a road I used regularly when I went with my sons to the beach. Though I must have passed by here a hundred times or more, I'd never once stopped to look at Saltwater Mansions, or at least not to pay it any significant attention. That there might be a story behind its door was true of any building. But not a story like the one I would soon learn.

Saltwater Mansions was a fine example of the kind of quietly breathtaking Victorian architecture often found in British seaside resort towns. It would be an impressive place to live. The kind of place where you'd closely watch your visitors' faces for signs of awe. Gentrification had changed Margate beyond measure in the thirteen years since Caroline Lane was last seen. Standing on the steps of Saltwater Mansions, I wondered whether she'd still recognise its faded splendour, or if it would only feel hauntingly familiar, like the face of a lost love appearing in a dream.

Grace had done me the favour of texting ahead, but I was nervous as I tried to explain myself to Dee through the intercom. I said that I wondered if I might be able to talk to her about Caroline Lane. Only now did I stop to consider how weird it might be to have a stranger arrive at your door wanting to discuss a missing neighbour. It had begun to feel like an out-of-character episode brought on by the heat. Floundering to right the situation, I told Dee I was just curious, that I could well be wasting her time.

Dee laughed. She said she'd been hoping someone would turn up asking about Caroline one day. It wasn't an inconvenience, she welcomed it. She loved talking about Caroline. For Dee, as for most of the residents of Saltwater Mansions, Caroline was the subject of an extraordinary obsession. Now that I had heard about her, how could I not want to know more?

The lock buzzed open. As I stepped inside I was relieved by the rush of cold air that escaped out past me, how it made the sweat freeze on my back. Making my way up to the top floor, I looked only fleetingly towards the darkness at the foot of the stairwell. A broken bulb hung above Caroline's door. I thought it might flicker. I was wrong.

Just as the outside of Saltwater Mansions featured some distinct peculiarities, the inside had the architectural logic of an Escher creation. Dee's flat had a strangely shaped staircase leading to a maze of adjoined bedrooms, and a children's playroom with a tiny, hidden door. From the lounge, a panoramic sea view of wind farms twinkling in the distance, like stars adrift on the water. On the walls were dozens of bright, surreal paintings. Her husband Carl was a keen artist. But it was their son who'd made the living room his own. A spongy, multicoloured play mat was spread across the floor, a parade ground for a disorganised squadron of superhero figurines.

Dee made us coffee and explained how her interest in Caroline began. The previous owner of her flat had been a director of the Saltwater Mansions management company, a formal organisation of residents who oversaw the running of the building. When he moved out, a vacancy arose. Dee grew up in Kent, so preferred to call herself a BFL, a back-from-Londoner, rather than a DFL, a down-from-Londoner, the nickname given to the gentrifiers by the locals. She was the type to roll up her sleeves, involve herself in her community and do what she could to improve things, so she immediately applied for the role. At her first meeting she was given a rundown of who her new neighbours were: a costume designer who primarily lived in London, a woman who worked in hospitality, an elderly couple, a few private tenants, and the lady in flat nine they said wasn't there, though nobody could explain quite why.

Dee's life was busy. She had a young son and they were working hard to make friends and settle in a new town. But whenever she had free time she spent it trying to find out anything she could about Caroline Lane. It wasn't easy. Caroline had no internet presence. Nobody who might have known anything about her ever came calling. And most of the neighbours only moved into Saltwater Mansions after she vanished, way back in 2009. Those that had met Caroline remembered she was quite a private person, though none of them had spent enough time with her to gain any meaningful insight into her character. By all accounts she wasn't an easy woman to get to know, even when she was around. Just as Caroline's disappearance was a mystery, so was the woman herself.

Except, there was this one thing. Dee slid a cardboard box across her dining table towards me. It was almost a foot high and close to bursting at the seams. Inside, she said, was something that, had Dee not rescued it to try and make sure Caroline wasn't forgotten, would have been destroyed:

thirteen years of Caroline's post. Every letter that had been pushed through her door since she left Saltwater Mansions and never came back.

Caroline's direct debits had remained operational, meaning she continued to exist, if not at home then in the circuitry of a bank's server somewhere. The humdrum mechanics of living, like the daily visit of a postman, had continued on in her absence. In this context, the box of post was an eerie, vaguely depressing testament to how much of modern life can be reduced down to the regular, automated transfer of money between one party and another, how that reads as presence in the same way we once considered locked eyes or the touch of someone else's skin.

There is a long biographical tradition of attempting to discern the truth of someone's life through their correspondence. While it applies more to historical figures than it does to someone who could feasibly have chronicled their breakfasts on Facebook, it was perfectly reasonable to believe that what was in the box might offer a glimpse of who Caroline was, and how she could have vanished into thin air without anyone seeming to notice. Dee smiled. She wanted me to have the lot.

I had worked as a journalist before, though I'm hesitant to use the term and do so only in the loosest sense. I'd never done any serious investigative reporting. Most of the work I'd had published in newspapers or magazines tended to be interviews with actors and musicians about a new film or record they'd made. Ironically, because of the constraints of time, modern public relations and the subject's general willingness to engage with their fifteenth interviewer of the day, it was usually almost impossible to tell their story – which was my job as I saw it – with any real insight or degree of depth beyond their recent experiences making whatever it was they were there to promote. I realised quite quickly that this could only be achieved if we were to sit down together for a prolonged period and they were to tell it to me. By and large this didn't happen. I was once sent to interview the band Daft Punk, but was given just fifteen minutes and only permitted to ask questions about a table they'd designed. So it was a frustrating endeavour I wasn't all that good at, and eventually I lost interest in trying. However, I knew how rare it was to chance upon a trove of documents like this, and I could immediately see how a clue to Caroline's story might lie inside it.

As I opened the box I felt magnetised; the hair prickled on my neck and arms. Dee had kindly weeded out the takeaway leaflets and junk mail that formed a sizeable percentage of the knee-deep, eight-foot-long, thirteen-year build-up of post behind Caroline's front door. But just as the absence of Caroline's story was what attracted me to it, it was what was not in the box that seemed to reveal more about her than what was, as though she existed in the negative rather than in the photograph itself.

In the thirteen years since she vanished, Caroline didn't receive a single birthday card. There were no Christmas cards. There were no letters from friends, no notes from neighbours. This didn't mean she was lonely or miserable. Perhaps these weren't things she courted or missed. She might have preferred a life alone. Solitude does not necessarily mean loneliness or a lack of fulfilment. But it was still sad to find nothing that spoke of connection to the outside world, to closeness or kinship, to family or love, all of these things evident in every corner of Dee's flat.

There was, however, one item of post that was very revealing about the kind of person Caroline might have been. At the top of the stack were the minutes of a meeting held by the Saltwater Mansions management company in flat sixteen one day in May 2009. The minutes were no simple record or list of the matters discussed, as you might normally expect to emerge from a meeting convened to discuss topics so dull as noisy neighbours and communal fire escapes. Quite the opposite. They were so comprehensive that it would almost be possible to recreate the meeting as though it were a scene from an uncomfortable play. A meeting that no one wanted to attend, not least Caroline Lane, three days before she was last seen.

Mr Peake was plumping cushions as if they'd wronged him when the first guests arrived, a few minutes shy of 10 a.m. He wouldn't describe himself as house-proud, but he liked there to be an order to things. Especially when he had visitors. And when they were on official business, as they were today, he wanted everything neat and tidy. Everyone needed to know he took his position as secretary of the Saltwater Mansions management company seriously. Even now, as the end he had hoped for veered into sight.

The Saltwater Mansions management company was run by the residents for the residents, but handling the day-to-day business could be a thankless task. Mr Peake had secretly wanted to resign for the past two years. It wasn't that his motivation had waned. He remained passionate about reducing the company's costs. Ensuring the building was properly maintained was why he got out of bed some mornings. And with Margate going to hell around them fast, it seemed doubly important to make Saltwater Mansions a nice place to live, on the inside at least. Nobody had any money and the streets were unsafe, especially at night. But the workload of the secretary was an unwieldy commitment, often undertaken at a financial loss, for someone like him, who had what he liked to describe as an unusual working lifestyle. If all went to plan, this would be his last Annual General Meeting. One of the items on the agenda was electing his replacement.

It seemed fitting that the passing of this mantle should take place in his lounge, over the fine selection of pastries he'd arranged on the table. Not that he'd had a choice other than to offer up his home. It wasn't like there had been any other volunteers. By and large, this had been the story of his tenure. So it would be his final inconvenience. And, though he did not know it yet, the source of a cancerous regret.

All those expected were present by the time the meeting was due to begin: Mr Peake, Ms Regis, Mr Sillett, Mr Curtis, Mr Pickering, Mrs Bennett, Mr Gynn and Ms Lane from flat nine. Their lacklustre greetings suggested nobody was particularly enthused to be there. Why would they? Mr Peake dutifully circulated the agenda beforehand and the items included flat eight's concerns about fouling in the car park. The almost supernatural abundance of dog shit that plagued Margate was one of many issues raised every year where no real progress was made. His joke at the 2005 AGM about digging spiked dog traps was met with frowns. Perhaps they'd assumed from his tone that he meant it.

Neither were they surprised by the footprint of Mr Peake's flat. Every property in Saltwater Mansions was bigger than it seemed from the outside. They had that in common. That and the walls between them when they slept. But plenty of the residents ignored the business of the management company, despite being at the whim of its decisions. So, by the mere fact of their attendance, it stood to reason that those present for today's AGM were bound by an interest in the common good.

After making sure everybody had a drink and was ready to begin, Mr Peake opened the meeting in the traditional fashion, by reading the minutes from the previous AGM. It was a dispiriting reminder of how little progress had been made since, but it was an obligatory one. Usually, this quick rehashing of old affairs passed without incident. But not today. When he'd finished, Ms Lane pointed out that the date of the 2008 AGM was missing from the copy of the minutes he'd issued to the members. Mr Peake, a stickler for detail, was mortified. She was correct. He apologised for his error. She requested a signed and backdated copy of the previous year's minutes, and he facilitated that while some of the others rolled their eyes. Protocol dictated that the group then agree this matter was dealt with before they moved on to the next item of business. And so a vote was taken. Did those present accept this new copy of the minutes as a true and fair reflection of a meeting held the year before? The 2008 minutes were confirmed as accurate by majority. Only Ms Lane abstained.

This was strange, but Ms Lane's awkward interjection was not wholly unanticipated by everyone. It was a sore subject, but Mr Peake had been forced to rearrange this AGM three times at her behest, effectively tripling the work involved in organising it. And Mrs Bennett had always considered Ms Lane to be a little bit odd.

Mrs Bennett had lived in Margate all her life. Witnessing the town's decline had been like watching the slow death of a majestic animal; an elephant bleeding out. Having resided in Saltwater Mansions for most of those years, four decades or more by now, she had a list of present and former neighbours that read like a telephone directory, and she remembered them all.

With most of them, a chance meeting at the back near the fire escape – that bloody fire escape, which would soon become the bane of their lives – meant making small talk and swapping gossip, a good old-fashioned moan about the expense of installing carpet in the communal hallway or some such nonsense like that. Mrs Bennett often found herself running late because of this kind of chit-chat and how long it was inclined to go on. But it was different with Ms Lane. There were no pleasantries. No small talk. Not even remarks on the weather. If Ms Lane laid eyes on Mrs Bennett or any of the other neighbours she would quickly scuttle off, closing the door of her flat behind her as she went. The clunk of the lock echoed through the stairwell like a gunshot.

Mrs Bennett could tell you all about the arguments Mr Downs had with his wife, Ms McGrath's demented dating history or Mr Phillips's secret pining for Ms McGrath. Saltwater Mansions was a hard place in which to keep a secret. But she barely knew a thing about Ms Lane. Now though, in Mr Peake's flat, something had changed. While Mrs Bennett might have predicted Ms Lane acting strangely, she'd never have guessed that Ms Lane wouldn't stop talking at all.

Mr Curtis, long-standing treasurer to the management company, scanned through his notes as Mr Peake moved the agenda on to point number two: the financials. The others listened carefully to Mr Curtis's comprehensive explanation of the company accounts and the past year's expenditure. He had a way with numbers learnt from twenty-five years in the armed forces, where he was taught double-entry bookkeeping. He'd developed quite the flair for it. In fact he was so good with numbers he did it for fun. Later in life, when he gave his own paperwork to his accountant, it would be so well organised he'd get a discount.

Though the figures for Saltwater Mansions weren't huge, the homeowners' money, and how much of it was collected, pooled and spent, was traditionally the AGM's biggest bone of contention. It was when discussing the accounts that living here felt most like being trapped in an unhappy marriage. Mr Curtis hoped this point of order could be swiftly concluded. Then they might move on to something more enlivening, like the matter of where Mr Peake's car was parked in the car park, which showed signs of subsidence at one end, and had concerned Mr Curtis for some time (as had Mr Peake's penchant for standing on the high wall at the end there, surveying the subsidence in those shorts he wore that didn't leave much to the imagination).

However, when Mr Curtis finished his short presentation, Ms Lane objected. She drained her coffee and made her wishes clear. The accounts should be audited by an independent third party. She didn't trust Mr Curtis, or anyone else present for that matter. And more than that, any future expenditure over £250 should warrant a letter be sent to all Saltwater Mansions homeowners, even though it would take up a considerable amount of Mr Curtis's unremunerated time. This wasn't their first run-in. Far from it. Ms Lane had questioned Mr Curtis's competence in the past, and he'd long considered her an arrogant piece of work.

Mr Peake had squeezed his mini pain au chocolat so tightly it was now roadkill in his palm. But he remained professional, confirming by a show of hands that those present saw no need to incur the additional cost of auditing the accounts, while informing Ms Lane that she was fully entitled, indeed welcome, to have the accounts audited if she was to arrange it at her own expense. After what Mr Peake diplomatically recorded in the minutes as an 'extended discussion', Mr Curtis's rundown of the financials was accepted by a majority vote of seven to one. The same numbers carried the next motion. And the next. And the next. In fact, all eight votes the committee held that morning fell the same way, including the vote to have Ms Regis succeed Mr Peake as secretary and put him out of his misery at long last. No matter what they were voting on, big or small, important or inconsequential, dog shit or drainpipes, seven carried the motion and one made their objection plain. Ms Caroline Lane from flat nine.

Years later, Mrs Bennett would remember the meeting as being so fraught it was abandoned after half an hour, but the minutes record it lasting over two. Perhaps half an hour was the point at which she started yearning to be back in her flat with her animals. Listening to Ms Lane prattle on had become almost intolerable. Not only was she contrary to every single consensus, every time somebody tried to reason with her she spoke at great length about her superior understanding of the law, or how she'd once worked in government in Westminster (the House of Commons maybe, or the Home Office, or the Foreign Office – years from now, nobody would be able to recall quite where). She complained that the company's directors should be changed, then refused to stand for the position herself. She objected to the election of five other directors, all of whom were in the room, turning puce. She argued against the standard payment of an honorarium to the secretary and treasurer, which wasn't the norm but would barely have covered the snacks on the table, let alone their time. Unless it was exactly what she wanted to happen, and who knows what that was, Ms Lane refused to let it pass. Mr Peake was pleased to note that their time, like his patience, was almost up. But they hadn't yet reached the trickiest matter of all. Item number eight on the agenda. The fire escape.

Unusually, Saltwater Mansions consisted of five adjoining blocks, across which were spread twenty-seven flats (for superstitious reasons there was no number thirteen). There were a smattering of communal spaces: the bins, the stairs, a small number of hallways. But the most significant shared area was the fire escape, an intricate network of metal steps and walkways that clung to the rear of the building and linked all of the flats together, looking more like the kind of structure you'd find on the townhouses in *West Side Story* than in impoverished mid-2000s Margate.

Now over a hundred years old, the fire escape was badly eroded and structurally unsound. In the event of a fire engulfing Saltwater Mansions (of the kind that at this moment Mr Peake might justifiably have welcomed or even considered starting), there were serious doubts it could hold the weight of all the residents at the same time without a collapse that would heap disaster on disaster. The building was technically unsafe. Without urgent action, Saltwater Mansions was at risk of being condemned. They could all be made homeless. Now, as a relieved Mr Peake sank back into his armchair, his successor appointed and his work almost done, Mr Curtis detailed their available choices, already sensing that Ms Lane was spoiling for a fight.

Option one: they could modify the flats, rendering the fire escape unnecessary and enabling it to be removed completely. He knew this was wildly unlikely. It would be a gargantuan job, insanely expensive, massively disruptive and entirely unworkable. But he'd learnt from his time in the military that offering three possibilities, starting with the most untenable – the nuclear option – might smooth the passage of the next two more feasible responses. They could replace the fire escape with a design identical to that existing presently, or replace it with a new design altogether. None of this would be cheap. And the cost would need to be split among the owners of all the flats, so it was also likely to be unpopular. But that didn't make it any less necessary. Bracing himself, Mr Curtis offered to obtain a quote for each option by the end of the month, from a military contractor he'd worked with before and trusted to do a good job.

Ms Lane was so incensed she seemed to levitate. The white heat of her ire for Mr Peake now turned on Mr Curtis. Were they to simply accept what he was claiming without scrutiny? Not on her watch. She knew the law. She'd worked in government. Mr Curtis despaired. The way he saw it, there was nobody more qualified in this room than him to talk about the fire escape. He'd been in engineering for years. He'd been personally responsible for the fitting of a brand-new hi-tech fire alarm system with a budget of a quarter of a million pounds. When it came to this kind of thing, there wasn't much he didn't know.

None of this mattered to Ms Lane. Without the gathering of further information and expertise, she would not countenance a word of it. A groan moved round the room like a raincloud. Nobody wanted to be at the bloody AGM, let alone attend more meetings. Especially during work hours. And besides, Mr Curtis was as thorough as he was competent. Surely adequate research had already been conducted on the issue?

Ms Lane didn't just disagree, she argued that Mr Curtis should no longer have the business of the management company registered at his home address, as it had been for convenience, and instead it should be registered at an office any of the members could access whenever they felt like it. This motion was voted against with a majority of four to one. Three of the members had already heard enough and made their excuses. Mrs Bennett wished she'd been one of them.

'Well,' Ms Lane said, 'I'll never use the fire escape, so I'm not paying for it.' This might have sounded unfair, or even just a straight-up dereliction of a leaseholder's obligations to the others in the building, but she was right. She would never use the fire escape. Just as the interiors of Saltwater Mansions had idiosyncratic floor plans, the layout of the flats within each block was also something of a puzzle. Ms Lane's flat, number nine, was on the ground floor. In the event of a fire, should she not be able to leave safely through her front door, she had any number of windows to exit through on almost any side of the building. Technically there was nobody safer. But the fire escape was listed in the leaseholder's contracts as a communal space, and so all residents were equally responsible for its upkeep, no matter their altitude when they lay in bed at night.

Mr Peake and Mr Curtis could see no immediate way out of this dilemma. Ms Lane had adopted a fervour on the issue that Mrs Bennett considered unsettling. Lunchtime was approaching, and this had been one of the more unpleasant mornings in memory, which was saying something, because Ms Lane had put them through a few. Mr Peake had no choice but to call the meeting to a prompt and merciful close.

Flashing apologetic glances at anyone whose eyes met his when Ms Lane wasn't looking, he showed the other homeowners to the door. His relief when it finally shut behind them was immediate. But his rage refused to dissipate. He allowed himself half an hour to gather his thoughts, before sitting down to type up the minutes in great detail while the meeting was at the forefront of his mind and his displeasure still hot.

It was another ten days before Mr Peake got round to writing his resignation letter, but time hadn't tempered his indignation. He was determined to make plain the reasons for his decision. Yes, he had been in the position of secretary for too long. Yes, he was sick of the work and the vacuum of gratitude he did it in. Yes, he was selling his flat (not that it was worth much these days). Margate's decline – the crime, the poverty, the shut-down shops with chipboard windows, the refugees, the drunks, used nappies fought over by gulls with pink eyes – it was all too much for him. He was old. He wanted a pleasant retirement. Somewhere clean and quiet and safe. Somewhere that wasn't here. But there was something else, something he approached on the page with an uneven mixture of frustration and restraint.

'The workload has been unnecessarily increased by quite an alarming degree due to dealing with the demands made upon Mr Curtis and myself by Ms Caroline Lane of flat nine, with regard to multiple issues,' he wrote. 'I acknowledge that Ms Lane has raised some valid points, [but] for the most part . . . I think it best for me not to specifically comment on the majority of Ms Lane's concerns.' He printed and folded twenty-seven copies of the letter, one for each flat, pleased with the sting in his penultimate paragraph. 'Throughout the last four years, Mr Curtis and myself have expended a great deal of time and energy into the running of the management company, which predominately has been a thankless task. In continuing in his role as treasurer, Mr Curtis has my profound sympathy.'

He slipped each letter inside an envelope and posted a copy through every single door in Saltwater Mansions. Starting with flat number nine, the ground-floor home of Ms Caroline Lane, where it would remain on the floor, unopened, for the next thirteen years.

Four

The following day I spread the contents of the box Dee had given me across my desk and started to read each letter over and over again, looking for clues. It was thrilling in the way that I imagined detective work to be thrilling. I hadn't expected to find myself in this position after going for a haircut on a hot day in June, but it now seemed reasonable to presume that I was, at that precise moment in time, the only person in the world searching for Caroline Lane. Or rather, searching for some trace of herself she left behind.

It didn't seem plausible to me that Caroline was still alive. Why would someone continue to pay the mortgage on a flat they hadn't visited for thirteen years unless they were dead? If Caroline was still alive, she must have a bank account full of so much money she didn't care. The alternative, that she was being held against her will, was almost too grisly to contemplate. The fact that nobody came looking for her and no one seemed to have reported her missing was bleak enough. The more I read, the more I became determined to learn about her. I didn't imagine that examining her post would reveal the truth of how she came to vanish, but it did seem to offer the only way to glean at least some understanding of who she was.

It would have been fanciful to hope that what was in the box would be as enlightening an insight into Caroline's character as the minutes from the AGM. In reality, the majority of it was no more revealing than a reminder she received every year to book an appointment at the opticians. Occasionally, though, I'd find something that might be pertinent. I discovered her middle name, which allowed me to be confident I'd found her birth records, using my father-in-law's login details to a website he'd been using to trace his family tree. These records in turn gave Caroline's date of birth (she would be fifty-eight now), and the names of her parents, Bert and Norma Lane (née Smith, which is unhelpful if your first instinct, as mine, is to Google things).

Using this information, I came across the one appearance Caroline makes on the electoral register. Bert and Norma's marriage records were also publicly available. But beyond that, I couldn't find any other mention of Bert or Norma in the National Archives. Even if I had, I'd probably be no closer to knowing who their daughter had grown up to be by the time she disappeared in the summer of 2009.

Neither was there any trace of Caroline online. She had no discernible digital footprint at all. At a time when even the most inconsequential parts of people's lives are recorded and shared, this only made the mystery more seductive. I've great admiration for anyone who doesn't have the minutiae of their lives splashed all over the internet. I see them as I might the survivor of a plague.

Having combed through the contents of the box multiple times that week, I couldn't escape the feeling that, if there were any clues to Caroline's story, they were in some way hidden in her absence. That the texture of her life lay in what could not be seen; in the shadow, rather than what cast it.

Mr Curtis tried many times to reach Caroline in the year after the 2009 AGM. It was an effort so frustrating he feared for his hairline. As promised, he posted through her letterbox a detailed breakdown of the work to be done on the fire escape and a quote for its cost, making it clear he'd be more than willing to discuss the matter, if that was what she wanted to do. There was no response. Nor did Caroline return her ballot when the rest of the residents took part in a postal vote, giving the go-ahead for the work to begin.

A short while later he sent an invoice for her share. It came to £2,380, to be paid by 1 October. Again, there was no response. Neither was there a reply to the follow-up invoice, to which Mr Curtis added a very British note that read 'polite chase-up', and asked that she pay with a cheque rather than her preferred option of a bank transfer. That way he wouldn't have to wait for his next statement to know that the money had entered the account, which always made everything a terrible palaver.

The deadline for payment was now fast approaching. Mr Curtis needed the money to pay the contractor so that work could begin before winter came. He knew from his military days that bad weather would make it a much tougher job to do. Cold knuckles, numb hands; if the frost bit it'd be all but impossible. Chasing payment from everyone else in Saltwater Mansions only added to his stress. Frankly, it was a task he wouldn't wish on his worst enemy. It wasn't just that there were others in the block with Caroline's lax approach to settling bills. There were some who couldn't follow even the simplest instruction. One resident sent his cash to a bank account he seemed to have plucked from thin air. Mr Curtis quickly grew to resent trying to organise everything late into evenings, when he'd much rather be relaxing in front of the television, and his frustration showed on his next invoice to Caroline in another particularly British way. The words 'polite chase-up' had been removed.

That winter, when construction was due to take place, was especially severe. But tireless work by the contractors meant that, against considerable odds, the fire escape was finished by the end of January, when a bitter North Sea wind whipped sleet across the town, leaving the sky a white and constant fuzz.

When it was complete, Mr Curtis slid another invoice through the door of flat nine. It came with a letter warning about the accrual of interest, and a request that reflected their past dealings as politely as he could muster: 'Please don't be stubborn . . . please be helpful.' He put his ear to the wood, heard the paper hit the doormat, and let out a long, tired sigh.

It all felt like a giant waste of time, but, following protocol, he sent a 'final reminder' shortly afterwards, warning Caroline that if she didn't pay her share immediately, as per company rules, he would have no option but to transfer the matter to a debt collection agency. Perhaps because Caroline was still paying the automated statutory annual fee of £500 for building maintenance that was required of all Saltwater Mansions homeowners, or perhaps because of a consensus already forming that she would never give in, or perhaps because it didn't matter what they did if she never responded, this threat never came to pass.

A year after Caroline disappeared, the 2010 AGM was a notably more sedate affair than its predecessor. Despite the glaring hole in the accounts, the everyday business of the management company had to trundle on. Those present agreed, and it was noted in the minutes, that 'the work [Mr Curtis] does for the company is exceptional, very time-consuming and very much undervalued'. They voted that his honorarium should be doubled to £400, then turned to other business.

One of the residents had died peacefully the previous Easter, so sympathies were extended to his family. Probate was put in progress, ensuring that any money he owed would be paid once his estate's finances were completed. Another flat was repossessed, its owner's debts to be settled by the mortgage company when the property was sold.

There were more maintenance issues to discuss. Some residents had raised concerns over how others were treating the dustbin area like a fly-tip for old clothes horses and spice racks. Complaints were made over antisocial behaviour. One flat in particular played loud music late into the night. It was agreed that all flats would receive a letter reminding them that 'consideration of other residents must be a priority, therefore making life more acceptable for all living within the Mansions'.

Another attendee spoke excitedly about the building of the Turner Contemporary on their doorstep. It was mooted to be a world-class art gallery, which seemed unbelievable to everybody present. Somebody remarked that it might change the town's fortunes. Gentrification! At last! Be careful what you wish for, said one. Nobody doubted these were interesting times for the strange place they called home.

Caroline's absence was discussed at the AGM, but only briefly. Mr Curtis gave an update so short it made the others laugh: they still hadn't heard from her. This might have been a source of great annoyance, but it wasn't a cause for great alarm. Beyond the fact that she wasn't there, to the people convened in the room there were no signs of anything especially peculiar. It wasn't unusual that the owners of flats in Saltwater Mansions weren't seen or heard from for long periods. Margate was a seaside resort town. Even though it had fallen on hard times of late, lots of people took advantage of low house prices to purchase cheap holiday homes. Prior to the advent of Airbnb and the influx of monied Londoners, they simply sat idle for much of the year. There were plenty of Saltwater Mansions homeowners who were only sighted in the summertime. It seemed perfectly possible that Caroline might have gone travelling, or that, wherever she was and however flagrant it appeared, she simply wasn't paying much attention to the bills for a fire escape back home. There wasn't really an awful lot they could do. They weren't her keepers. She hadn't even wanted them as friends.

If any of the residents reported her missing, it either wasn't mentioned or was never recorded in the minutes. The general feeling was one of futility and resignation. What might the police have done, other than enter her into a database of missing people to which another name was added every ninety seconds? There was no evidence of a crime having been committed. Nobody had noticed anything untoward. Caroline might have disappeared, but it didn't feel like something had happened so much as something hadn't. It was as though they'd heard an echo when there had never been a sound.

In many ways, Caroline's presence was still felt. Mr Curtis experienced a bolt of tension ricochet through his chest whenever he passed her door. This lasted right up until he retired as treasurer a few years later, after which the accounts were less scrupulously managed, and the cast of the Saltwater Mansions management company quickly changed almost entirely. The residents who didn't die, or have their flats repossessed during the town's leaner years, capitalised on the increasing value of their homes, sold up and moved on. Others took advantage of the rise in demand for rental property. They bought new out-of-town places for themselves, and enjoyed the regular passive income paid by their tenants. Those few who played the game right found themselves quids in.

Soon, only Mrs Bennett remained from the class of 2009. With her neighbours went the first-hand memories of Caroline and the way she behaved that day. Her mentions in the minutes faded to footnotes, then to nothing. But for the unpaid cost of repairing the fire escape, and the incremental rises to the maintenance fee, neither of which were the subject of an automated bank transfer, her absence might have gone unnoticed. Were it not for the ceaseless drip of mounting debt, Caroline Lane might not have been missed at all.

It would be eleven years after that meeting before a new incarnation of the Saltwater Mansions management company reviewed the hole in the accounts and finally took action. In spring 2020, an ominous letter landed on the huge dune of post behind the front door of flat nine. It was from Milton Volks Solicitors. They had been instructed to inform Caroline that she now owed over £13,000 in maintenance charges. And unless she paid in full within two weeks, legal action would be taken. Caroline could lose her flat.

Of that fee, £2,380 was for the fire escape maintenance, which had been completed over a decade previously. The bulk of the rest of the remaining overdue payments was for work carried out on the building in the intervening years, though since solicitors had been instructed to chase the debt, legal fees were being accrued too. Saltwater Mansions had had its exterior repainted twice. Structural work was carried out on the sinking car park. The leaky roof had been fixed. There was a new front door, and a number of minor repairs. The cost for these had been split between the owners of the twenty-seven flats, all of whom would grumble about it at one time or another.

Mrs Bennett, thought to be the last person to have seen Caroline alive the day before she disappeared, might have found her exasperating, but she had to give her credit for being true to her word. She'd told them she was never going to pay for a fire escape she'd never need to use. They didn't expect her to vanish, but at least she hadn't lied.

When there was no response to the solicitor's letters, the Saltwater Mansions management company looked at the debt and the further maintenance needed on the building, and used their AGM to vote on whether to take legal action. This was both a last resort and a complicated undertaking. But if they wanted to recoup the money and be able to pay for future repairs, they now accepted they had no choice. Owning a flat in Saltwater Mansions bound them to a communal project. If Caroline wasn't willing or able to contribute, something drastic needed to be done.

At the height of summer 2021, Canterbury County Court issued a claim form in which the figure owed, having accrued fees, interest and court costs, leapt to over £19,000. Caroline did not respond. Nor did she to notice from Milton Volks sent a few months later which stated that unless they received payment of a sum now totalling more than £20,000 immediately, their clients, the Saltwater Mansions management company, would seek a court order for the forced sale of flat nine. Outside Caroline's kitchen window, streaks of rust appeared on the fire escape's metal banisters, a copper-red trail glittering in the midday sun.

*

In order to force the sale of a property, a claimant must satisfy the court on two counts. Firstly, that they have reason under law. Which the Saltwater Mansions management company did: the debt. Secondly, that every conceivable effort had been made to contact the homeowner. In Caroline's case, there were precious few avenues to explore. They'd sent letters. They'd knocked on her door. They'd done everything they could beyond forcing entry to the property, which might have constituted a criminal offence. They'd no reason to suspect she was dead inside it. There was no stench of rotting flesh. No meat flies. No bloodstains blooming like fetid poppies on ceilings, walls or floors.

Mindful of doing their due diligence (and motivated by their own intrigue, since Caroline's fate had become a topic of near-constant discussion among the neighbours), the Saltwater Mansions management company called in the professionals. They didn't want to be halfway through the sale of her flat only for her to walk back in one day and derail the process. That would cause them terrible trouble. So they found an agency that specialised in tracking down people who needed to be found. Caroline fitted the bill perfectly. A hunt began.

Typically, the agency looked for people who'd skipped town with a debt to pay. People in debt were never especially hard to find. Usually they'd only been uncontactable for a few weeks and were not that far away as they had nowhere else to go. More often than not they were holed up in the home of a lover or family member, hoping their transgressions would blow over eventually, their punishments inexplicably waived. But in Caroline's case, she'd been absent for so long that the work was more like that of a private detective on a cold case. After so much time had passed there were few solid leads to follow. In fact, there was only one.

Despite claiming to the other members of the 2009 Saltwater Mansions management company that she worked in the heart of government, Caroline only appeared on the electoral register once. For a few months in 2004, she lived on Britain's west coast. She was forty then, and staying with her mother and father. Every theory the neighbours swapped was conjecture at best, but it was easy to frame this as the result of a break-up or divorce. That Caroline was with her parents for a brief period of respite, getting her affairs in order, before rebuilding her life and finding a new home. And that this, purely by coincidence, is what she'd been doing when it was time to register to vote. She moved to Margate a few months later.

One morning in the autumn of 2021, the man from the agency yawned as he and his colleague made their way down the narrow front path of this seaside address. It was an inconspicuous, middle-class home on a quiet road, with trees lined up either side of the garden path like soldiers by the coffin of a fallen comrade. Seventeen years had passed since she was known to have been there. If they weren't devoid of hope that they'd find her, there wasn't much of it to go round. Still, their job was to chase leads, and this was all they had.

What they didn't know is that they weren't the first to knock on this door in search of Caroline Lane.

Ruby was Dee's neighbour, and another present-day resident of Saltwater Mansions who'd become obsessed with finding out what happened to Caroline Lane. On the rare evenings when she wasn't working her hospitality job, when she was cooking or running along the seafront, Ruby loved listening to true crime podcasts and watching documentaries. Her only problem was that there were almost too many to choose from. She never knew which to start next.

In the ones she enjoyed most, the mysteries weren't cracked by a detective with a badge. They were solved by ordinary people. You didn't need to be Poirot or Sherlock Holmes if you had internet access and a nose to smell a rat, because widespread use of social media and easy access to public records proliferated the tools that meant anyone could find out almost anything about anybody. The once-hidden lives of others were fair game.

As the mystery of Caroline's disappearance brought their little Saltwater Mansions community together, amateur sleuthing became Ruby's new hobby. She too found Caroline's sole entry on the electoral register, before the agency was even aware of her existence. Noting down the address, she hatched plans to convince her friends that they should holiday near there one weekend. When she revealed why – she was chasing down a lead on a mystery – no one hesitated to say yes.

The others hid in the car while Ruby tiptoed round the outside of the house, glancing through the windows, trying to get a feel for the place. It seemed perfectly normal. Lived-in. Pleasant. Fine. Only then did she stop to ask herself what was she expecting. To find an amnesiac Caroline sunbathing in the garden, as though she'd banged her head and forgotten her old life like Goldie Hawn in *Overboard*?

Suddenly, a man emerged.

'Can I help you?' he said. Ruby thought fast.

'Is this the place that's for sale?' she asked. The man smiled.

'Oh, no, that's a bit further down the road. People get confused all the time.'

He dropped his bag of rubbish into a bin and pointed her in the right direction. She apologised for bothering him and walked up the path, gravel crunching loudly underfoot. Back at the car, her friends were giggling. Why didn't she just tell him the truth? She felt foolish now, but she hadn't wanted to spook the guy. Imagine how freaky it would be to have someone arrive at your door on an otherwise ordinary afternoon, searching for a woman who had vanished off the face of the earth.

On their own visit two years later, the staff from the debt collection agency drew a similar blank. The resident told them he'd only moved into the address five years previously, and had no relationship whatsoever to a Caroline, a Norma or a Bert, who he presumed must have owned the house many years before. He seemed so confused by their line of questioning that they were convinced this was true. They thanked the man for his time and drove back to their office satisfied there were no more threads to pull. Their search, they felt, was comprehensive enough for a judge to rubber-stamp the sale of Caroline's flat. And they were right. They didn't need Caroline's consent any more. Even if she suddenly reappeared, the flat and everything in it could now be sold, donated or destroyed.

Caroline's homeowner status officially came to an end soon after. At the beginning of winter Canterbury County Court issued a hand-delivered notice which, if she'd ever opened it, would have informed Caroline that her eviction from flat nine Saltwater Mansions was to take place in exactly one week's time. She was to leave the property with all her belongings before the clock struck ten.

But when the bailiffs came she wasn't in. And you can't evict someone who isn't there. After the legal proceedings were over it fell to the Saltwater Mansions management company to arrange the forced sale of Caroline's flat. Finally, they could go through her door.

Five

One afternoon in the middle of August, I was playing a board game with my sons when Dee rang. It was around six weeks since we first met, and we'd kept in touch almost daily via WhatsApp, but she had never called before. I sprang up from my seat and answered immediately. I'm not sure she even said hello before telling me she'd finally found a copy of a video recording she made on her old phone of the moment when she and the present members of the Saltwater Mansions management company entered flat nine, thirteen years after Caroline left it for the last time. The minutes from the 2009 AGM might have been weird, Dee said, but it was this recording that cemented her obsession. The video she was sending me now.

The last words Dee said to me on the phone looped in my head as I pressed play. As with Caroline's story, what was most striking about her flat was not what was there, but what wasn't. There was no dust. There was no dust because there'd been no skin.

It was early January, a month after Caroline's absentee eviction, when the Saltwater Mansions management company's latest incarnation finally got the keys to her flat. The five present members – Dee, Ruby, Bert, Janet and Mrs Bennett, who, after a lifetime in this building, had nothing new but this to see – huddled expectantly outside the door. Dee suggested she should film them entering, just in case they found anything. She didn't need to say it any more explicitly than that. They all understood she meant a body. The corpse of Caroline Lane.

No one truly believed Caroline was dead in there. Wouldn't they have discovered it by now? But they'd been waiting too long for this moment, thirteen years in Mrs Bennett's case, and none of them were immune to the effects of all the gossip, theories and stories about Caroline they'd shared. Whether they dared admit it or not, their imaginations had been fired up in irrational ways. Plus, it was dark. The bulb had blown. They all felt spooked enough not to rule it out.

Dee tapped her phone screen a few times until the camera pulled focus on Bert's hand as he slid the key into the lock. She let out a short, involuntary shriek, only just audible on the recording beneath her quickening breath. Her enthusiasm for filming gave way to a deep unease as the door opened. It felt like entering a tomb.

On the floor of the hallway was a knee-deep pile of post roughly two metres long. Bert pushed a path through it until they were all inside. Despite everything they knew about Saltwater Mansions' peculiar floor plans, they were all taken aback by the flat's size. An architectural quirk of being on the ground floor meant there was simply more of it. The corridor that ran through the middle was wide and airy, like the kind you might find in a school. There were spacious rooms on both sides, a high ceiling and alcoves full of bright winter light.

To the left was a door. Here, in the first room, was nothing but an ornate, gothic four-poster bed made of intricately carved dark oak. At each corner was a candle, perched on its own elegantly whittled wooden stand. It felt more like a staged scene from a haunted house than somewhere a person might actually sleep. The kind of bedroom viewed from behind a rope. The thought that it was a sex thing crossed a couple of minds.

Bert picked up a framed photograph from the bedside table. It was of a woman in a summer dress with white spaghetti straps on lightly tanned skin. Partially obscured by long, light-brown hair, her face was curiously unreadable, lips curled upwards slightly at the corners. Was this the beginning or the end of a smile? Her eyes skewed right, away from the lens, but the photo didn't appear to have been taken spontaneously. It was posed. She'd chosen to look away, as though she didn't want anyone to study her gaze.

Bert showed the picture to Mrs Bennett. She was the only person who might be able to confirm this was Caroline, even if, by her own admission, her memory of what Caroline looked like had become hazy in the years since the 2009 AGM. Mrs Bennett nodded, remarking on how the photo was both intimate and distant. This was also how it had felt to meet her. Like you'd remember her forever, but never really know her at all. Dee's goosebumps rose. To her it seemed time had stood still. That the flat had been sealed. That they shouldn't be there. She thought she might be sick.

Had Janet not known better she'd have sworn the kitchen had been in use only moments before they arrived. It wouldn't have surprised her if the hob had been warm to the touch. Beneath a framed poster from the Hayward Gallery, crisp white vests hung from a clothes horse, about to be folded. Dirty plates rested in the sink, waiting to be washed.

The oven door hung open like a slack jaw, as if to cool. There was food in the fridge, rotten now of course. Janet said it was as though Caroline had been abducted by aliens. Mrs Bennett joked that they wouldn't have wanted her.

On the kitchen countertop was a personalised calendar. Each month featured a different photo. It must have been made for her as a gift. Eerily left open on the page for May 2009, the month she disappeared, the picture showed two young children sitting on the knee of a woman, her hands around their bellies, her face enveloped in shadow. A sister perhaps. Young nieces who'd be women by now.

In the next room, Caroline's bedsheets still held her shape. Her clothes were spread around the head of the bed, a mosquito net stowed above it (for decoration, they presumed). The wardrobe was packed with a collection of outfits, the kind Janet could only dream of. Caroline owned maybe seven or eight pairs of leather trousers. They weren't the cheap type, Ruby noted. All quality. And they weren't the kinky type either. More the yes-absolutely-if-you're-brave-enough-to-wear-them type. She liked Caroline more by the second.

Hung beside the trousers was what Janet assumed to be a British Airways skirt. She remarked that it might have been part of an air hostess's uniform. Mrs Bennett had no recollection of Caroline saying she was an air hostess. But after all these years spent wondering about the contents of flat nine, to now be confronted with so much stuff was overwhelming, and she could no longer be sure if her memory was serving her well. She didn't dwell on it. Nor did she envy Janet. It would be Janet's job to oversee the sale or disposal of all Caroline's belongings, with all the money made going towards her debts. But it was an imposing task. This was a lifetime of possessions, each item imbued with unknowable meaning, an unheard story, an unwitnessed existence. The rocks her comet collected as it streaked briefly through the sky: a pair of wool-lined slippers, a padded jewellery box, a burgundy leather suitcase. This was what remained of Caroline Lane. A book about nutrition unread on the bedside table, a doll of the character Big Ears from Enid Blyton's Noddy books, still in its cellophane wrapper. It would take a week or more to sort through.

While the bedroom and the kitchen felt lived-in, the next room seemed strangely bereft. It was big yet empty but for a rug, a fan, a round table, four chairs and a computer that had long since slipped into obsolescence. Dee assumed it was the dining room, though its bare, cold walls suggested that in here few meals had ever been served.

She felt more comfortable in the lounge, where she found signs of what was once a life. There were three or four clocks and two telephones, and almost all the furniture was made of wood. Wicker or bamboo, from Malaysia maybe, or Bali, or Indonesia. On the coffee table in the centre was a tall glass vase full of fake white roses. On the wall an opulent, egg-shaped mirror. On the bookshelf books about travel, some in other languages, Italian and Spanish. And a compendium of artists: Cézanne, Gauguin and Turner. Outside the window, the glorious Margate sky the latter made his muse.

Ruby went into the bathroom and screamed. It was dark with the blinds drawn, but in the darkness was what appeared to be blood on the sink. Blood in the bath. Blood spattered in circles on the floor. She had long been convinced that Caroline's disappearance involved violence. If not physical then psychological or temporal. Some grim manifestation of the threat Ruby felt whenever she walked home late at night, or went jogging down the coastal path most mornings, or sometimes simply waited for a bus.

It wasn't until she turned on the light that she realised the blood was hair dye. A solitary rubber glove dangled from the tap, and as Ruby examined it she began to calm down. Caroline didn't die here. But she did change the way she looked. And she did so in a rush. Ruby might only have been an amateur sleuth, but she couldn't escape the idea that when Caroline left this bathroom all those years ago, she'd urgently needed a disguise. There was something she was hiding from. Something so intolerable that vanishing had been her only choice.

While Bert called a local estate agent and Janet divided the clothes into piles labelled donate or sell, Dee scooped up the post, filing it into a box, knowing that if she didn't it would all be disposed of or destroyed and there would be even less sign of Caroline left behind. It took an hour but it was worth it. There was no other way for her to leave flat nine with anything resembling a feeling of hope. She wanted to believe that someone would come looking for her, that hidden somewhere in thirteen years of one-way correspondence was a clue to the woman Caroline Lane had been before the end, whatever the end was. Before all of this. It soothed her to believe we don't live unseen, that all lives are indelible. That our reflections stay mirrored in the eyes of those we love.

None of the people who entered flat nine that morning left without forming an impression of who Caroline might have been based on the things they had found inside. And they didn't differ all that wildly. In fact, they mostly overlapped. The Caroline of their shared creation was cultured. She was snooty. She was independent. She was interesting. She was insular. She was elegant. She was, in some profound way, apart. Caroline might not have been there, but the version of her that existed in their minds was so vivid it almost felt like she was still a neighbour. They would all think of her nearly every day for months and years to come.

Watching the video again, I attempted to build my own mental image of Caroline Lane. But while I wanted to try to ensure her story wasn't forgotten, there was a distinct limit to what I could know of the truth from the handful of facts I'd discovered: a record of her behaviour in a single meeting, and a glimpse of the things she'd once owned. If I were to imagine Caroline, she would only be a projection of who I wanted her to be, little more than a character in a story about her that I was telling myself because it was what I needed or wanted to hear.

Caroline steps off the train at Margate station, soothed by a calm sea that greets her like a kiss. She loves going to London. If you ask her, not that anyone ever does, ambling around galleries is a fine way to spend a Saturday. Art is up there on her list of beautiful things. Second only to travel. She travelled a lot as a young woman. Paris, more than once. Southern Italy. Last-minute, sun-baked Lisbon. And, oh, the Caribbean. When she closes her eyes she can still feel that treacly stepping-off-a-plane warmth just beneath the surface of her skin. Travelling's been the engine of her closest relationships. The ones that stick in the mud of her dreams.

But as much as she loves London, she adores returning to the coast. Its salt-spiced, lip-stinging air. The cat-hiss of waves breaking. Good weather helps, obviously. Margate seems to have its own ecosystem, its summers a fraction hotter than it feels they ought to be, like a naughty child testing the boundaries of what it can get away with. She loves her flat, too. It's peaceful. It's hers alone. And in its own way, once the door is closed behind her, it's perfect. She walks homewards along the seafront, keeping her eyes on the familiar loveliness of the shoreline rather than the parade of amusement arcades that garishly illuminate the way.

Inside the canvas bag hanging from her shoulder is a print she bought from the gift shop. She longs to be surrounded by art; the paintings of Modigliani, the literature of Proust. These things that fill the belly of a life. Other than the AGM tomorrow, the bloody AGM with those bloody people, she has a relaxing weekend to look forward to. At some point she'll hang this print among the others, framed on her living room wall, or in the kitchen maybe, above the drying rack.

Caroline walks everywhere quickly. She walks home quickly now. Sidestepping the groups of young men who seem to linger on the steps that lead down to the sea all day, mumbling and smoking cigarettes. Beyond the ocean, the sky and the beach, Margate has precious little about it that she appreciates. So many of its buildings have fallen into disrepair, and what glamour the town was once famous for has been scorched by the sun of barren summer seasons and neglect. There are deeply engrained social problems. You don't have to look far to see them. Chaotic drunks straggled about the bus shelter. Pug-faced teens making trouble on the harbour arm. Overflowing bins. Dog shit – so much dog shit. People lost to worlds of their own, their prone bodies stuck in this one, a world that has failed them completely. Ugh. God forbid.

In the process of buying her flat she shared her fantasies with the estate agent. That Margate would soon undergo extensive regeneration. The area would change. The estate agent wanted the sale so indulged her. He knew her type:

cut-glass accent, brusque phone manner, whiff of disdain when he'd offered instant coffee. He knew which buttons to press.

These things he promised her. A blossoming arts scene. Well-lit, clean streets. Decent shops for buying wine. No matter that she wasn't a big drinker. Just a glass at the end of the day, or two at the end of a hard one. Bars a lone woman can go to and feel safe in. And cafes that do a good brunch. Poached egg on sourdough, avocado – avocado! – and grilled vine tomatoes.

He got that right. Caroline never eats junk. No hunger can drive her through the door of McDonald's. She craves decent restaurants. Like the French bistros in Soho where she'd seen out her twenties. Dim sum in Mayfair. The green leaf salad at the Covent Garden Hotel. She'd been casually rude to waitresses in all these places. That's not to say she's rude. Not all of the time. She can be sharp-witted. Funny. Contradictory, a jarring marriage of naivety and confidence.

She's a brilliant conversationalist. She's forthright and opinionated. She's fully engaged, always; if she likes you that is. And for that honour you need manners. Intelligence. Taste. A knowledge of politics (ideally left-leaning, though not too far, a quiet blue vote on occasion, hmm, in the middle she might say). Caroline's affection is hard won. The same is as true of people as it is of food. She never lowers herself. Never. Not for brunch, not for lovers, not for anything.

There's a warm pink dusk squatting on the esplanade when she arrives back at Saltwater Mansions. She hopes none of the other residents are in the hallway collecting their post. No sign of anyone. Her lucky day. She slips into her flat unseen. Kicks off her shoes. Makes a garlicky pasta. Then flops down on the sofa, steam dancing over the plate. But for the low hum of BBC Radio 3 from the kitchen (a joy to hear Aram Khachaturian's Masquerade Suite), it is quiet here. Bliss, to be shut away from the bustle of Margate, surrounded by the things that bring her such pleasure. This music. Her vases. Language studies textbooks. Ornaments reminding her of Africa.

She leafs through the newspaper she picked up at Victoria and started to read on the train. *The Sunday Times*, its supplements well thumbed in this order: culture, style, news. Her television is small and rarely watched. When she does have the misfortune to catch a glimpse of reality TV, or her eyes accidentally move over the racks of celebrity magazines at the newsagents, she despairs. Who could possibly enjoy this shit? It's enough to bring on a loneliness she lifts with a deep, hot candlelit bath, a glass of red wine and a good novel. Sometimes it seems such a tawdry world.

No wonder she's happiest in her own company. No wonder she's dreading the AGM. The small-mindedness of it all, its nit-picking business, the forced marriage of neighbours with nothing in common but what – bricks?

Muscles softened now, wine weighting her blood, Caroline wraps her hair in a towel and slowly makes her way to bed. Sleepiness brings down her guard enough for introspection. These last few years living alone in Margate, where she feels like an alien every time she steps through her door, she's really got to know herself. OK, she isn't everyone's cup of tea. Yes, she can come across as difficult. Snobbish maybe. Unfriendly. Direct (she thinks this a positive attribute, though she's aware from experience that others do not). But she is determined, and focused. She knows what she wants from life, and that there isn't enough time left to spend doing anything she doesn't want to do. And why should she? She built this life for herself. Through necessity. Through volition. A nice flat full of nice things in a town far away from her past. If she was to disappear here, no one would ever know. All she'll leave behind are these nice things.

Six

Towards the end of August we booked a cheap, last-minute holiday to Lanzarote. The food at the resort was terrible and there were cockroaches, but it had a huge pool and an inflatable doughnut that kept our children occupied, giving Lou and I some much-needed respite after what had been a difficult few months.

The restaurant boasted fine views of a starlit harbour. When Lou caught me staring into the middle distance over dinner, she suggested it might do us both a favour if I think about something else for a while. She was right, but I didn't admit it, and I couldn't really stop. Caroline Lane was never less than intensely present in my thoughts.

Some nights I waited until Lou was asleep and the only sound was the creaky song of cicadas. Then, in bed, lit blue by the rectangle of light from my phone, I would search the website for the UK Missing Persons Unit of the National Crime Agency. Tortured by her unfinished story, I'd think about how Caroline might have died.

One bleak possibility, the first that came to my mind and the one I thought most believable, was that she'd taken her own life. According to the minutes from the 2009 AGM, her behaviour in those final days was erratic. The evidence was by no means comprehensive, certainly not enough to glean any three-dimensional understanding of someone's mental state, but it would not be beyond anyone who read them to imagine the way she acted as being indicative of significant personal problems, something deeper and far more catastrophic than an issue with the restoration of a fire escape.

If what she said and did in that meeting were the sputters of an engine before its explosion, it seemed she had no one to turn to in her moment of need. Nobody beyond the walls of Saltwater Mansions had come looking for her since she disappeared. Mrs Bennett said she had no friends. Nor had she demonstrated any willingness, or ability, to make them. Caroline lived a solitary existence in a flat overlooking the ocean, where, every year, an estimated 200 people take their own lives. Tragic though it may have been to speculate, it wasn't out of the question she'd waded into the water and never come back.

It seemed less plausible to me, but there was a chance she was still alive. If I could believe something awful loomed over her to the degree that she'd taken her own life, I also had to be able to believe she had escaped it by running away and never coming back. Whatever horror she'd wanted to run from can only have been big and fearsome for her to go for this long. It must have been intolerable for her to completely jettison her life. Though her disappearance was mysterious, if this was the case, I hoped wherever she'd gone to she found enough distance from her past.

Of course, neither could I discount the grim prospect that she'd been murdered. Crime rates in Margate were spiking in 2009. The town was suffering severe social breakdown, reaching levels of school failure, addiction, teenage pregnancy, mental health crisis and unemployment that rivalled inner-city areas considered rife with deprivation. Not that such things only happened in troubled places. Picturing Caroline's name being added to a long list of women killed by men in this country in what amounted to an epidemic of violence sadly wasn't too great a stretch.

By dint of the fact that she never opened them, and the closeness of the meeting to her disappearance, it seemed likely the minutes of the 2009 Saltwater Mansions management company AGM was the first item of post pushed through Caroline's door after she vanished. It was reasonable too to assume that notice of Mr Peake's resignation was the second letter of any note. Sometimes, when I let my imagination run away with itself, the suspicion that he had played a part in her disappearance woke me in the middle of the night.

On one level, it all made sense. The resignation letter was essentially a signed record of his motive, and the time between the meeting that went wrong and Caroline's last sighting was conceivably short enough to be something other than coincidence. If I intended to kill a neighbour over a petty grievance, I'd like to think I wouldn't post a letter about how much they got on my nerves through their door just before I did it. But everyone's different. It couldn't be ruled out that Caroline had been the victim of some unspeakable act, or that somebody horrible had escaped the consequences of a heinous crime. If this was the case, it urgently needed redressing for all manner of reasons, not least achieving justice for her.

It'd be dishonest of me not to acknowledge here that, on a few occasions, I indulged in a fantasy about being the one who brought the perpetrator to justice. My aim might have been to make sure Caroline's story wasn't forgotten, but – as embarrassing as it is to admit – there was a dark allure to this kind of conspiratorial thinking; the idea that, from the shadows she left behind, I might drag the truth into the light.

It was a fantasy bolstered by my writerly ego. But there was a cultural aspect to it too. It reflected something I'd noticed before I'd even heard of Caroline: a fundamental change in the way we respond, and the right we think we have, to what we don't know about the lives of others.

I don't like aligning myself with the kind of person who, when they come across a mystery in the life of a stranger, spends their time online making videos where they speculate about what they really think happened, as though the truth was being purposely hidden, and they, and only they, might be the one to crack it. I find the idea distasteful and conceited, and seldom done in the interests of its subject. But while it wasn't for public consumption, in many respects what I was doing wasn't all that different. In reality, I knew nothing concrete about the circumstances surrounding Caroline's disappearance. Anything I said about it was simply conjecture. Like a conspiracy theorist reading into the evidence things that aren't there, every supposition threatened to pull me further from the facts, towards the telling of a terrible fiction. One that might be dangerous, or ethically unsound to invent.

By early September, when our holiday was over, my preoccupation with Caroline had become a hindrance in many aspects of my life. I devoted the hours I should have been working to poring over her letters for any details I might have missed. I made elaborate spider charts to gather information in a way that might reveal hidden patterns. Entire working days were lost to dreaming up new variations of search terms and trawling websites with even the most tangential of connections. I wrote long posts in forums for people nostalgic about pre-gentrification Margate in case someone there remembered her. I emailed pleas to the Home and Foreign

Offices to see if anyone there remembered a colleague named Caroline Lane. They were all ignored.

One evening Lou paused the film we were watching to point out that I'd spent the first half of it on my phone scrolling through the Facebook pages of women in their twenties with the surname Lane. I was forced to admit I'd been doing this in the hope I might somehow chance upon the young girls in the photo on Caroline's calendar, who I'd decided were her nieces, as though I might recognise them now they'd grown up from the brief, pixelated glimpse I'd had of what they looked like as children. Lou shook her head.

'Do you actually think one of them might mention Aunty Caroline in their profile?' she said. I felt a pang of sheepishness, but I wasn't deterred.

There had been many times in the previous four months when Lou had patiently entertained my devotion to finding out more about Caroline. I worried it might bore her, but if it did she never let on. On the contrary, she found my intrigue intriguing. Lou was of the belief that, had I heard about Caroline at any other point in the thirteen years she'd been missing, I might have mentioned it to her later that night, and then moved on the next day. I would certainly never have left Grace's salon and gone straight to Saltwater Mansions, just like most people in those circumstances would never have left Grace's salon and gone straight to Saltwater Mansions. In Lou's opinion, I just happened to have stumbled on Caroline's story at the right time for me to want, or need, to lose myself in it. 'You were open to it,' she said. 'That's why.'

A few weeks later Dee and I had intended to go for a walk, but the weather was too dismal. Rain lashed the windows of Saltwater Mansions, so instead we stayed inside and watched the violent heaving of the sea. Dee got up to make coffee, and while we waited for the kettle to boil I asked what brought her to the building in the first place. We'd never stopped talking about Caroline long enough for me to ask her anything so personal before.

Dee told me that she grew up a few miles down the road in Herne Bay. She and her husband Carl were friends as children. They attended the same primary school. Though they lost contact as teenagers, they were surprised to bump into one another at art school in London, where eventually they got together on a Thursday evening that felt more serendipitous than most.

These were good times. Partying in their tiny flat. Going dancing. Working stupid jobs. Having no memory of the night bus home. Nothing really mattered while they had each other; they could lose entire weeks to boredom and being in love, to painting and making dresses, to doing nothing at all. It was all too much fun for them to notice life was getting serious. How nights out turned to nights in, spontaneity to forethought, locked arms to held hands and tongued kisses to pecked lips, in the same gentle, understated way that summer turns to autumn. They built careers and got married. It was the wedding they'd dreamt of. In the photographs Dee's hair was pink and Carl's smile wide. They gazed through a blizzard of confetti into one another's eyes.

Only when their son was born did it begin to feel they'd outgrown the lives they'd built for themselves in the city. London rents were too high and the places they could afford too small. It made sense to move somewhere they could have space. Somewhere that, when they inherited some money from Carl's father after his death, they could finally afford to buy a place of their own. They chose a life by the sea.

*

Not so long ago they'd never have considered Margate. They remembered it from their childhood as being violent and grimy, the punchline to a joke about a place you'd never want to go. And for good reason. After its tourism economy crashed in the 1980s, the town struggled with widespread social deprivation. Many of the businesses that were forced to close when their customers disappeared left behind hollowed-out industrial units. With a stack of plywood and some judicious paintwork, they were easy to turn into large studio spaces. More crucially, they were cheap to rent. Painters, sculptors, writers, poets and musicians were all traditionally people without much cash. Moving to an impoverished area like Margate meant they could both develop their practice and eat without the patronage of wealthy parents, which would almost become a prerequisite of a career in the arts by the time the Saltwater Mansions management company finally gained access to flat nine.

Artists weren't the only people who needed affordable places to live. There were bohemians and single mothers too. Juggling childcare with paid work meant they'd willingly move to places like Margate; places where people with choices and money (the two being indivisible) wouldn't go. This first wave of gentrifiers weren't homeowners likely to benefit from the effects on their investments. In fact, the impact they were having would ultimately lead to their displacement; they'd been making a bed they wouldn't get to sleep in. But because they'd brought their cultural capital to town, they plumped the pillows for those who would. It was these artists and bohemians and single mothers who began shifting the perception of Margate from run-down and rough to vibrant and edgy, a vital change in optics for what was to come next.

It was in the neighbourhood of Cliftonville that the second wave of gentrification could first be seen transforming the landscape. Lou and I, who were renting a tiny house in the Old Town and trying to keep a baby alive, arrived at the beginning of this process. We watched the DFLs snap up the crumbling former guest houses and turn them into huge family homes with chequered-tile porches, slate-coloured Farrow & Ball paint jobs and ornate gold numbers on the doors. Their value rocketed at freakish rates. It was all anybody seemed to talk about in pubs.

The DFLs lobbied the local council to clean up tired parks, spruce up waste collection and pick up dog shit. They opened cafes and galleries and bars. Like Plinth, which sold art. Cliffs, a coffee shop with a sideline in vinyl. Transmission, a record store. Or Urchin, an off-licence-cum-exhibition space that sold expensive wine in the heart of one of the most deprived areas of the country, where poverty, alcoholism and addiction ran rife. In Urchin, a friend of mine once watched someone perform a poem about taking cocaine.

The DFLs weren't just altering the appearance of the place. They were beginning to redefine its very nature, making the streets and parks and businesses around their new home reflect their middle-class tastes and serve their needs. It was good news for those who believed in the progressive values gentrified communities typically shared. There would soon be growing movements aimed at protecting the environment – a particularly prevalent issue on the coast – and promoting diversity and inclusion. Margate Pride would quickly become one of the country's most popular celebrations of queer culture.

Hardly anyone could have disputed that Margate needed change, but the locals can only have wondered what was happening to the town as each new organic grocery shop or yoga studio further whittled it from what they'd known into somewhere altogether different. Rents rose beyond their ability to pay them. Bars they couldn't afford to drink in opened. Shops they couldn't afford to buy food from appeared. The outlook became disproportionately bad for the poor and people of colour, displaced by an 'arts-led regeneration' whose proponents talked a good game about investing in their community, but whose schemes and businesses in practice tended mostly to benefit people who looked and sounded like themselves.

In October 2015, a month after we moved to Margate and a week before our baby was born, Cliftonville was named the fourth most deprived area in the country based on factors such as unemployment, health care and educational achievement. By the council's own admission, issues like crime and the high number of vulnerable children were being managed rather than resolved. In the week that I found myself sitting on Dee's sofa while rain battered the windows and she carried on telling me her story, *Time Out* magazine named Cliftonville 'the coolest neighbourhood in the UK'.

When Dee and I spoke about the sad possibility that Caroline might have run away, and what horrors she might have been trying to escape, Dee remembered the best advice she ever received from her father, Edward. He'd told her more than once that if you don't deal with trauma as it comes to you in life, it will only haunt you the next time you have a problem and it will be bigger and more than you can handle. Always try and deal with your problems as they arise, he said, because they don't ever really go away.

One irony not lost on Dee is that, while she had been trying to assemble Caroline's story, she'd also been doing the same for her dad. Edward was diagnosed with dementia around the time that Dee moved into Saltwater Mansions. As devastating as the news was, it made her return to the area seem all the more timely. If she could be near him, she could care for him. She could try to harvest his memories before they were lost.

Up until the age of fourteen, around the time she lost contact with Carl, Dee's life had been enjoyably staid. She lived in a picturesque stretch of suburban Kent, with both parents and her brother and a bunch of close friends she'd hang out with most days. It was only in adolescence that everything started to unravel. This was when her father told her that the family life she'd enjoyed was an illusion he'd stage-managed to keep her from learning the truth. And the truth, it turned out, was more awful than she could begin to imagine.

Dee never knew it, but her mother had experienced protracted psychotic episodes throughout her teens and twenties, and again after she'd had children. Doctors believed these terrifying splinterings of self to be linked to violent fluctuations in her hormonal make-up that occurred naturally in puberty, young womanhood and childbirth. Now entering the menopause, she was having another, this one more severe than the last. Edward had navigated these difficult episodes before, but it had come at great personal cost to his own health. He didn't have the strength or stamina, the well of love necessary, to do it again.

Their marriage failed with terrible timing. Dee's brother learnt of his parents' plans to divorce just before he left for university, where Edward wouldn't be able to check on his welfare. Struggling to cope with the upheaval, he'd had a falling-out with their mother, gone out one night and taken acid. The comedown was devastating and, away from his family, he'd tried to take his own life. All of this, Edward explained to a teenage Dee, had given rise to a deeply buried personal trauma of his own. There was something terrible and seismic in Edward's past he'd never spoken about to anyone before. Not even his wife when she'd been sound of mind. One day, when he was ready, he hoped to be able to tell Dee what it was.

Years later, as the dementia gripped and their closeness intensified, Dee realised this was her final opportunity to hear what her father had waited so long to say. She spent every moment she could asking him questions about his life and recording his answers. Sometimes they didn't make sense. Sometimes the process became too sad for them to continue. But occasionally he'd reveal a little of himself, and she found she was able to build a life from the pieces, in a way that reminded her of sifting through Caroline's post. So she committed herself to knowing his story. To making sure that it was told.

That afternoon in Saltwater Mansions, when the wind howled like an animal wanting to be let in, she started to tell it to me.

Seven

Edward Smithson's father Jack told his employers at the bank that he was going to die. They asked him where he and his wife Rita would like to spend his remaining years, but he hadn't really given it much thought. That would mean accepting death as a grim inevitability rather than an inconvenient formality, something to sombrely inform his boss about. But he'd been to Torquay as a child and remembered it fondly. The long, golden beaches. The peaceful, tree-lined coves. So Torquay was his answer. He would move from London to Torquay in Devon, and the bank would thank him for his years of service by helping his family to relocate. They would live and he would die by the sea.

Jack didn't share the news with his son Edward. He only told him they were moving. Edward was excited, right up until it dawned on him that his brother and sister had other ideas. Mary, who was twenty-one, thirteen years older than Edward, refused without a second thought. No way was she leaving London. She was going to stay in Sheen and get married. Billy, the middle child, eleven years older than Edward, couldn't imagine living in the middle of nowhere any more than Mary could, not now that he was a young man with his whole life ahead of him. He announced that he was going to join the army, despite problems with his health in the past, the awful business of a burst appendix that had almost finished him off. Jack and Rita worried themselves sick, but Billy was an adult. He was capable of making his own decisions. So that just left Edward, all alone.

Jack and Rita had one final appointment before they moved to the coast. It was a meeting they had grown to dread more than death itself. Jack's parents, Bob and Diane, lived in a village called Sunningdale, near Ascot. It was built around a single straight road, a canal of cement with houses either side. Bob and Diane's house was behind a white picket fence, where a thin path wound through pristine lawns towards the building, which was squat and handsome, the brickwork so clean it seemed to glow.

They arrived at midday. Edward and Billy were made to sit in the kitchen while their parents spoke to their grandparents in the lounge. They rolled an apple across the table to one another and tried to catch it when it wobbled off. Edward didn't know what his father was saying in there, but the sound of crying coming from the room next door wasn't like anything he'd heard emerge from a human being before.

Billy heard it too. He took Edward by the hand and led him away from the sound through the garden to the woods enveloping the back and the pond that in the shade was as black and still as oil. There, as far as they could get from the house, Billy showed Edward the dragonflies, how they hovered and twinkled like emeralds. He put an arm round his younger brother and told him something that at eight he couldn't fully comprehend. Then he held him and said that it would be OK, that one day in the future he would understand completely. They sat together in the long grass, their legs touching now and again.

Later, when it was time to leave, Diane took some coins from a hanky she used to wipe tears from her eyes. She handed Edward the money through a gap in the fence and tried to smile for him, her lips curling upwards then dipping, like a bird not yet able to fly.

Billy was posted to Hanover at the beginning of 1953. Because of his medical history, the army wouldn't let him be a soldier, so they put him in the catering corps to cook for soldiers instead. Edward spent those first few months in Torquay pining for his brother. He daydreamt about Billy all day at school and late into the evenings, when he'd stay out until sundown, walking, digging in the dirt and finding trees to climb, places he'd remember to show Billy as soon as he came home.

When Billy was due back on leave, Edward and his mother hung 'Welcome Home' banners all around the house. Edward waited by the window with his hands pressed against the glass. Even his father, who barely moved at all these days because of the pain from the kidney disease, couldn't quite contain his excitement. Just as it began to feel like the wait might kill Edward, there was a knock at the door. He bounced over the sofa and reached it before his mother even got to her feet. But it wasn't Billy. It was the postman delivering a telegram. It said Billy was seriously ill in hospital in Germany. And then there was another telegram two hours later. That one said Billy was dead.

Edward's parents tried to cope using silence. It was as though a mountain had appeared in the garden and nobody dared speak of it. After Billy died, Edward never heard his name said by anybody, ever again. But Edward vowed to never stop talking to Billy in his head. When he went on his walks he'd talk to Billy about nature. He'd climb trees and describe the view. He'd say, *Billy, where are you? I miss you. When are you coming home?* He didn't need any friends because he still had Billy. Billy was always there.

Most days, Edward stopped off at Torquay beach on his way back from school. On this day he picked up a rock and watched the insects beneath it scuttle into the shadows. Afterwards, as he made his way back for tea, he told Billy all about them and the way it seemed the shade had sucked them from the light. He came through the gate and up the path and it was weird because the front door had a window either side and usually his father was in the left one. He'd see him on the sofa. If he was awake he'd wave. But today he wasn't there and the door was open. Edward went in through the door and found his dad lying on the floor in a pool of blood. There was blood coming out of him, his nose, his mouth and his body. Dripping in places and gushing in others. Haemorrhaging out of him, pools of blood, a river on the floor.

He went to his father and his father said, 'Edward.'

And Edward said, 'Daddy.'

And his father said, 'You look after your mother.'

His mother who'd gone to get help. Now he understood it. That's why the door was open. This is what he was thinking about – what a funny thing to think about, why the door was open – when his father died.

Jack died thirteen weeks after Billy, and thirteen weeks later Edward's grandfather Bob died too. His mother never said it was a broken heart that did it. That he'd lost a son and a grandson and it killed him. She said it was old age. But Edward, who'd lost all three male members of his family in twenty-six weeks, never liked the number thirteen after that. He developed all kinds of superstitions. Grief turns the air to ash, but time moves through it anyway.

The bees were bobbing for pollen and Edward was on the front lawn waiting for Billy to walk in through the gate when he heard a raspy voice say his name. He looked up and saw the old woman who lived next door. There were two old women next door, and his father used to say the other was bedridden. Edward could barely imagine how scary she must be, given how terrifying he found the sight of the one who could actually walk around. Her skin was white and thin, blotched with constellations of liver spots he thought must be the plague. She reminded him of a turtle.

'Hello,' she said. 'How are you?'

He looked towards the gate, for Billy.

'Would you like to come over for some tea?'

Edward froze. But his mother appeared in the doorway and encouraged him to go, quietly thanking the old lady for this act of kindness that was being transmitted on a frequency only she was hearing, as Edward reluctantly followed her up the path next door.

They sat beside the bedridden lady upstairs and drank tea. He'd never dare touch her. What if his hand fell through her skin and spiders came out? But he grew less afraid as they ate sponge cake. Then the old lady said, 'I know there are a lot of changes in your life right now. But there is a circle to life, and you have to look at the little things, the little creatures, to understand how it maps out.' She placed her teacup on the bedside table and produced a small stack of books about British moths. They weren't all brown like he expected them to be. Some were colourful and exotic and flamboyant, their wings patchworks of pinks and greens and blues. One reminded him of a peacock's tail feathers.

The old lady said she was a scientist. He wasn't sure if she'd written the books, but he was excited when she told him he could take them back to his house to examine more closely. He took the books straight to his mother and excitedly explained that he needed to learn to read and he needed to do it fast.

It had been too long since Rita last saw his smile. And this was the first time he'd ever been enthused by a book, no matter how hard she'd tried in the past. So she called a woman she knew who used to be an English teacher and made arrangements for Edward to see her next week. Until then, he would have to be content with looking at the pictures. And he was. He was entranced by the colours and shapes and fragile beauty. The forewings and hindwings and thorax, intricately constructed around one another like the innards of a clockwork watch.

Now that he wasn't scared of the old lady any more he spent the next morning sitting on the grass in the front garden with the books, for once not watching the gate for Billy, but the fence for her so that she might invite him round for tea again and they could talk about what he'd seen in the books. Then a hearse pulled into the road and stopped outside her house. That's when he knew for sure, this dark power he had.

Edward wasn't long into his entomology PhD when he was invited to a dinner party. He took his classmate Neville, who talked about leeches. The other guests there might have thought Neville strange but Edward found it riveting. So did Belinda. She was an entomology undergraduate he'd not met before. Like Edward, she was especially keen on lepidopterology: the scientific study of moths. Edward thanked his lucky stars he'd ended up at Swansea University and finally found people who carried a magnifying glass around with them all through their childhood too. In Belinda and Neville he had friends for the first time in his whole life. But Edward still spoke to Billy every day. He told him all about his PhD and moths and his romance with Belinda, which was only just beginning and filled him with warmth.

Whenever they had a spare weekend, Edward, Belinda and Neville went hunting for the fabled Blue Underwing. The Blue Underwing was a rare British moth and a lot of lepidopterologists considered it the holy grail. Edward had never seen one, but he'd been obsessed with it since the day he first opened the old lady's book. They were hard to track. Their numbers were dwindling. Though rumours of sightings sometimes moved through the mothing community they were usually unreliable, and more often than not there was no way of getting to the location of a sighting quickly enough to confirm either way; by the time you'd heard the news they were gone. If you did catch one, you'd see it had a twelve-centimetre wingspan and a spectacular bright-blue stripe across its black hindwings, that the marbled effect on its forewings made mesmeric shapes from light when they yawned open in the morning sun. Its scientific name made perfect sense to Edward. The 'Clifden Nonpareil'. It meant 'beyond compare'.

One afternoon in October 1966, Edward drew the short straw. Neville unfurled a large map on the kitchen table, Belinda tied a blindfold round Edward's eyes, and Edward slammed a pin down into it. Wherever it landed, he would have to drive them there. They'd then find the closest woodland, where they'd set up camp and spend a couple of nights in search of the Blue Underwing. It was an exercise in courting dissatisfaction maybe, but at least they had each other. Edward was pleased to learn his pin had landed just forty miles from Swansea. It was about an hour's drive. Not too far away. They would go that night.

Edward's radar for the desires of others wasn't all that finely tuned. So he didn't notice Belinda and Neville getting closer on the back seat. Maybe he should have done. It must have been plain to some degree – in a few years' time, Belinda and Neville would marry and have children and go on to be together for more than five decades. But on that drive Edward could think only of the Blue Underwing, and this strange, unpleasant sensation he began to experience as they pitched their tents near the woods in heavy rain, as though he was being pulled towards the trees. It was a feeling new to him, discomforting but compelling. He didn't know how to articulate it to the others, so instead he told them he was going to set some moth traps and made his way into the forest. The sky succumbed to darkness and their laughter entwined in the distance behind him like the lilting notes of a harp.

Edward walked up the hill until he neared the middle of the woods, where the branch-dappled moon cast a clearing in milky light. The pull was stronger here. As he reached the trunk of an oak, Edward found he couldn't move his feet. He looked down and saw the brambles beneath him were spindly fingers now, winding round his ankles, grabbing him, holding him still, forcing him to look at the bark on the tree, which was shifting and moving and dripping like blood. Like his father's blood. Welling in the cup of a knot and forming Billy's face in the wood. Billy's face made from their father's blood, opening his mouth now to speak.

Belinda and Neville were surprised by the speed with which Edward wrenched up his tent from the mud and bundled it into the car. There was wildness in his eyes and it frightened them. They tried to dissuade him from leaving but he was already starting the engine. They wondered if maybe he'd caught them kissing. But Edward couldn't care less what was going on between Belinda and Neville. He just wanted to get out of there. He couldn't get Billy's warning out of his head.

The next morning, back home in bed, he was woken by his radio alarm clock. He made a cup of tea stronger than he usually took it and listened to the news. His face was gaunt, his skin with a distinct bluish tint of its own, and though he heard what the newsreader said it didn't quite go in.

On a slope above the mining village of Aberfan was a colliery spoil tip thirty-four metres high. It had collapsed that morning and slid down the hill as slurry, engulfing Pantglas Junior School and a row of houses down below, crushing and killing 116 children and 28 adults. Death had rained down from the hills above, where Edward sought a rare moth in the woods, just the night before.

Billy didn't speak to Edward again after that. Or if he did, Edward could no longer hear his voice. He wondered if it was because he hadn't stayed and listened to his brother. What if Billy had wanted to tell him what was going to happen so that he might stop it? What if he lured him there because he wanted Edward to die too, so that they would be together and neither of them would ever be alone again? Instead, Edward had turned his back and run away, and now his brother had vanished forever. His best friend Billy was gone.

Predator and prey relationships were what interested Edward most. The interactions between two species, where one is the hunted food source for the other. The circularity of it. Wasn't it just like the old lady said? That life could be chaos, a series of random events, any one of which might upend it at any moment. But there was comfort in understanding life as a loop. That the end is a hand held out to the beginning. That the beginning holds in it the end.

He'd taught predator and prey relationships among insect species to thousands of students from all over the world from the University of London's Kent annexe, the specialist entomology department he'd helped build into an esteemed institution. Some would have thought him eccentric, with his bald head and huge beard and the handkerchief full of coins he kept in his pocket. But they were entomology types, so they considered Edward wise and clever, warm and honest. No one knew about the dark curse he carried with him everywhere he went.

There was a section of the M25 that Edward couldn't bring himself to use. It was on the west side of London, so if he needed to travel from the south-west of England to the north-west, and that route involved taking the M25, he would drive counterclockwise around it, adding close to 100 miles to his journey. This was the only way he could think to guarantee he wouldn't see signs for Sunningdale, the village where his grandparents had lived, because even seeing the word written down made his throat tighten with fear. It would feel as though he couldn't breathe.

One day Edward's boss informed him that they were dismantling certain parts of the university and selling it to other universities. The entomology annexe, he said, was to become part of Imperial College London, which already had an entomology annexe in Ascot, which was where he'd be doing his work from now on. Edward fought the urge to vomit. There'd be no avoiding that section of the M25 now. Not if he wanted to pay the bills. Not if he wanted to keep doing the job that he loved, that he had worked his whole life towards.

He kept his eyes firmly on the road on that first day. If he so much as saw the familiar green of a road sign approaching he brought his focus back to the car in front. He managed to arrive at the university without any nasty surprises, but it was clear this wasn't a workable solution. If he drove like that whenever he made the trip he'd be crushed beneath the wheels of a truck. Over a sandwich that lunchtime he told himself he had to face his fear head on.

By the day of his next lecture, he'd summoned the courage to drive through Sunningdale, albeit at speed and without looking at the houses either side of the long road that scythed it in two. And by the next, he found he was able to slow down and try to spot his grandparents' house. Though he remembered the house, remembered looking up at it, remembered the fence, he couldn't recall where it had been on the street, couldn't see one like the image in his memory. The village hadn't changed much, and there didn't appear to be any new houses. Perhaps it had been knocked down; sold and levelled and built over, all trace of his grandparents' past ground into the dirt.

The cafe on the corner wasn't new either. He had a vague recollection of it which became more vivid as he walked through the doors. The menu hadn't changed but for the prices, and on the walls were scores of black and white photos of the local area, specifically the school at the end of the village and the children who used to attend. He examined the photographs as he waited for his breakfast. One of them, up so high he had to crane his neck to see it, was a class photo – three rows of kids interspersed with teaching staff. And right at the back, with his arms proudly outstretched as though these were all his children, was the headmaster. His grandfather, Bob.

Edward hadn't remembered this was Bob's job until now,

and was astonished to learn that the information had been lurking, unknown, in the furthest recesses of his mind. He wondered what else was there. Suddenly he found he could name his grandparents' house, and his hand trembled so violently he had to lift his cutlery in the air to stop it rattling on the table.

'Excuse me,' he said to the cafe owner as she collected his plate. 'Would you happen to know the whereabouts of a house called Sandhalls?' She'd been here as long as the cafe but Sandhalls didn't ring any bells. It'd been a long time since the villagers had used house names over numbers. She suggested he try the church. The vicar there was a mainstay of the village. When it came to local history there wasn't much he didn't know, and there were precious few of the people who'd lived in Sunningdale over the years he hadn't met.

Months passed before Edward felt brave enough to visit the church. Sometimes he'd drive through the village as though he might, then change his mind at the last minute and go home. He was scared the vicar might have answers. The sight of his grandfather's face on the photographs in the cafe had been enough to make him take to his bed for a week. And yet he kept returning. Driving past. Slowing down. Speeding up. Stopping once or twice, when he knew the church would be closed and there was no one else around.

One cool autumn morning, when he saw the doors were open, Edward took a deep breath and walked in. The vicar was not expecting visitors, but the sight of a stranger was welcome and he smiled. Edward approached, his footsteps echoing off the floor. As he opened his mouth to ask the question, an older lady with tightly curled hair appeared from behind a curtain into the sanctuary. She saw him and froze, her hand clutched to her lips.

'You're a Smithson, aren't you?' she said. 'There hasn't been a Smithson in Sunningdale for almost fifty years.' Edward couldn't speak. He ran out of the church into the graveyard, which was vast and overgrown. A young couple were carrying boxes up the path towards the church, so he hurried round the rear of the building and hid in the shade. He stayed there until he could no longer hear their voices, and while he waited he looked across the graveyard. There were hundreds of gravestones all around him, and many more lost to the undergrowth. They were not all tall and legible. Most were rectangular, thin stones, barely two feet long and eight inches high, so they were swallowed by the grass and it was almost impossible to read their inscriptions. But not ten paces away he could just about make out a name he recognised. His own name. Smithson.

He knew his grandfather must have been buried here somewhere. Bob had lived his whole life in this village. This was where he'd died. But the sight of the grave, blackened with filth, made him sad in ways he'd not expected. He knew that if he didn't try to tidy it up, no one ever would. He got down on his hands and knees and began to peel back a great clump of turf from its side, thick wedges of compressed mud coming away from the stone to reveal a brilliant white. And as he tugged and pulled and the turf came free, he found an inscription, beautifully carved into the marble. Here lies Smithson. Here lies Jack Smithson. Not his grandfather. Not Bob Smithson. Jack Smithson. Edward's dad.

The soil was turning to blood on his hands, dripping down his fingers. The earth turning to blood. Pools of it, all around. His father beneath him now.

Edward ran through Sunningdale as fast as he could. He ran until he could run no more. So he was staggering, clutching his hand to his chest, when he saw the house across the street. Suddenly, everything fell away. The new wood. The new bricks. The new glass. All of the changes and extensions that had been made to the building since he had last stood here and his grandmother had passed him the coins from her purse fell away until he saw in his mind the house as he remembered it. This handsome, squat house that in the sunlight seemed to glow. He crossed the road and plunged his hand into the hedgerow. His skin scratched open on the thorns until his fingers reached the picket fence inside.

'You're welcome to come in,' the man said. He was suited and clean-shaven and his eyes were the green of an under-ripe lime. Edward yanked his hand from the hedgerow and stood up straight so that the man wouldn't think him as crazy as he felt. Had he mistaken Edward for someone else? The man gestured to the sign in the front garden. 'For sale. Open house.'

Edward followed the man up the path towards the front door. The man showed him the lounge where his father had explained to his parents that he was dying. He showed him the kitchen where Edward had heard them crying as he rolled an apple across the table to his brother. They looked at the bathroom and the bedrooms and the stairs, and Edward couldn't shake the feeling that he was still here somewhere, that his eight-year-old self might leap from a cupboard. If he wanted, the man said, he could check out the garden. Edward opened the door and stepped outside.

Billy's hand felt so big. He hoped that when he got older, his hands would be exactly the same. Billy showed him the ponds and the dragonflies. They walked as far as they could from the house, Billy's arm round Edward's shoulder. If he had known this would be their final conversation, that, after this, Billy would go straight to the train station and then the airport and then to Hanover, what might he have said? *I love you. Don't go.* Or perhaps it would have played out just as it did, with him saying nothing at all. Can you swim against the currents of a life?

'There's going to be all this change,' Billy said. Edward didn't know what he meant. He just didn't want him to cry any more, not like all the old people back at the house. But he listened as Billy said, 'There's going to be all this change. Because, you're moving. And Mary, she's going to get married. And me, I'll be going away. So there are going to be all these changes.'

He always listened when Billy spoke. Even if he didn't know what he was talking about, it still went in and stayed in there. Stored until the future, when he needed it most.

'But you don't need to worry about anything. We'll always be together. You and me, Edward. We'll meet in these gardens again in fifty years.'

Decades later, when his past was fading from his recollection and before it was too late, Edward told this story to his daughter Dee. The two of them walked hand in hand through Hanover's military graveyard, sombre in black against tooth-white stones. A short brush of manicured grass. Straight lines in the soil. All this loss.

They fell at Billy's grave and wept, Dee for her father, Edward for his brother. They wept in the rain, the blood, the memory, his story washed away.

Eight

It was a blustery late-September day and the air was tinged with the scent of crisping leaves when I finally got to speak to Mrs Bennett. She still lived in Saltwater Mansions, but arranging to meet her had been complicated. Now retired, she was a full-time carer for her husband. Mr Bennett was in poor health, and she was understandably cautious about picking up any illnesses, especially since the pandemic, so they didn't leave the flat much, if at all. Chatting to a stranger about a woman she'd never really liked, didn't know very well and hadn't seen for almost a decade and a half was an unnecessary risk whichever way you cut it. However, as she was the last person in the building to have seen Caroline, I was keen we might be able to come to a compromise: a quick chat in the car park, where we could remain a few metres apart.

I watched as she slowly descended the stairs of the contentious fire escape, seemingly impervious to a raucous sea wind. Mrs Bennett was a small woman, with a weary stoicism that reminded me of a bison fronting out a blizzard. There was a sharpness to her eyes not blunted by age.

'I don't see so much of the neighbours these days,' she said. 'Not since the pandemic. It's harder to keep track of who they all are.' That difficulty had only been exacerbated by Margate's regeneration. The resultant demand for property sped the turnover of residents. Older owners were keen to offload their homes as prices spiked, and a queue of newcomers from London were happy to pay good money. 'It feels like every week there's someone new next door.'

Lockdown wasn't all bad. It had fostered a sense of community that had been lacking from Saltwater Mansions for some time, if not in the traditional sense. Mrs Bennett, Dee, Ruby and a few of the others set up a WhatsApp group. It was supposed to be so that they could look out for one another, but it was mainly used for gossip. They sent each other messages about the arguments in flat twenty-six and a certain neighbour's suspected extramarital affair. Most of all, they swapped theories about what might have happened to Caroline Lane.

As the only remaining Saltwater Mansions resident to have met Caroline, Mrs Bennett was an anomaly. She'd seen a lot of people come and go, more than she could count, and it was near impossible to recall how many AGMs she'd sat through, interminably discussing debt and drains and all the other boring business that comes with living in a block like this. But never in all her years did she meet anyone quite like Caroline. As far as she was concerned, everything I told her was recorded in the minutes rang true. It wasn't just Caroline's erratic behaviour that made her memorable, though. There was something else. 'A weird feeling,' Mrs Bennett said, 'that one day I'd hear about her again.'

The way Mrs Bennett saw it: her time left on earth was limited, and she'd rather spend it on people she liked than on the former owner of flat nine, whom she always found difficult and strange. But she still thought about her often. How could she not? The agency hired to find Caroline might have thrown in the towel, but Mrs Bennett still looked out on her flat from her kitchen window every time she did the washing-up. Its emptiness haunted the building. 'I suppose if the professionals couldn't figure out what happened,' she said, 'what hope is there for anyone else?'

The wind had picked up and Mrs Bennett began to shiver. I asked if, before she headed home, I might quickly read her the list of names of the people in attendance at the 2009 Saltwater Mansions management company AGM, just in case it prompted any more memories about the time around Caroline's disappearance. She agreed. Most of them were people she hadn't had cause to think about in the intervening years. She'd no idea what became of some. Others she knew to be dead. There was one, though. She hadn't heard from him in a long time, but she was quite sure that Mr Curtis emigrated to New Zealand a few years ago. 'Possibly, and I might be mistaken, for love. I think he even got married. I think her name might have been . . . Maggie.'

Mrs Bennett apologised. She was glad that someone was interested in finding out what happened to Caroline, and wished me luck, but she wasn't sure how she could assist me any more. She had to get back to her husband and her dogs.

Afterwards, I sat in my car listening to the recording of our conversation. It was of terrible quality. I'd owned the dictaphone since before Caroline disappeared from Saltwater Mansions, and its old microphone had been unable to handle the distance between us, how softly she spoke, or the way the wind whipped her voice from her lips as it left them. Thankfully our conversation was still fresh enough in my memory that I was mostly able to piece together the things she said from what words it was possible to make out. Before I drove home I jotted down what I could in my notebook, underlining anything of interest, even if I wasn't sure exactly why that was the case.

I'd been so focused on finding out what Mrs Bennett knew about Caroline that I'd not really paid much attention to something else she said. It was little more than an aside, a bit of small talk. But it struck me now, when I saw it on paper. As she'd left to return to her flat, Mrs Bennett mentioned how amused she was that anyone would point a dictaphone in her direction at all, irrespective of the mystery of Caroline Lane. 'I can't think why anyone would want to record me saying anything,' she said, laughing. 'I don't have anything worth telling.'

I wrote that down and thought about my father.

My parents' house, where I grew up, where they still lived, was a thin corridor of small rooms that got smaller every time I came home. To get to the back of them, you'd need to pass through the others in sequence: front room, living room, kitchen, bathroom, each traversable in five short steps. In the centre of the living room in the centre of the house was Dad's armchair. The leather had worn where his head came to rest. It looked like a halo. I didn't visit often enough, but when I did I enjoyed watching my sons play on the rug at his feet. How he'd pretend to steal their toys. How they'd try to get them back. Their laughter seemed like an echo of my own.

It was just the two of us that evening in November 2018. I was amazed that the boys, Lou and my mother could sleep through the noise of fireworks outside. The sky strobed through gaps in the curtains and the air felt rich with trouble. Dad said it was like a war zone out there. He'd said this every 5 November of my entire life. I'd never much cared before. To me it sounded like the grumble of an old man whose ears rang with tinnitus from sleeping next to the engine room on a ship. But now I had children of my own, one of them an eleven-month-old baby it had taken an hour to get to sleep, I found myself in firm agreement. We laughed about how our thoughts might be aligning at last as he lowered himself into his armchair and winced. Either I was catching him up or he was slowing down. Probably it was a little of both.

It was rare to find him sitting still for long. He was a restless man who liked to work. Since leaving the navy he'd been an electrician, a security guard, a dog handler, a patio layer, a taxi driver and a school caretaker. Sometimes he did two or three of these jobs at the same time. The concept of slowing down in retirement proved unpalatable, so when the time came he started doing odd jobs for local pensioners as though he wasn't one of them. He'd drive neighbours to and from hospital appointments. He'd repair their broken toasters. He'd test their burglar alarms. Once, he arrived at an old lady's house to find she had lied to him. Nothing needed fixing. She just wanted company, because she was lonely and knew him to be kind.

Word travelled fast around Nuneaton that Keith Whitehouse was a man who got things done. Soon he was receiving calls from friends of the people he had helped. Could he change a lightbulb? Could he do their shopping? Could he fix a microwave? He bought a second-hand mobile phone for this purpose, a broken handset held together with worn elastic bands, and he would answer at any time of day or night. I'd seen him leave Christmas dinner to help someone. A cold oven. A raw turkey. Him, pushing his chair back from the table, pausing only to kiss my mother goodbye.

Dad had a visceral dislike of talking about himself. Better, he thought, to be judged for his actions than by his words. Looking back, I can find myself wondering whether this was because he came of age at a time when men revealed little of their inner lives. The Second World War was still more news than memory, and the realities of his upbringing made Nuneaton a place hostile to self-interest. His family didn't have much money. Work put food on the table, not self-aggrandisement or anything so conceited as that.

But there was some deeper foundation to his lack of self-regard, a fierce adamance that his story was not worth telling, as admirable as it could be frustrating if you wanted to know what it was. If you'd asked him, he'd have told you: 'What is there to say?' He was the man who'd knock the wall down for you if it was in your way. Who'd drop a tin of soup at your door when you were sick. Who'd clear your guttering or scare off your bully or fetch your bread. He was a doer and he'd do what needed doing, not look back to see what he had done.

As a child I'd been unaware that my father had had a life before I was born. As a teenager I'd been disinterested. As a young man I'd been too wrapped up in the construction of my own future to trouble myself with his past. But since becoming a father I'd been bothered by the idea that my sons might one day ask me questions about their granddad's life that I would not be able to answer. And worse, that I had never really sought them. I didn't know his story. I had a terrible recurring dream that, when he died, I would not be able to write the eulogy he deserved. I'd begun to grieve the conversations we hadn't had, but what pained me more was that I didn't know how to start them. We were, in his mould, not ones for deep conversation or introspection on the subject of each other or ourselves.

It was for these reasons that everything I knew about the crash, I'd learnt from my mother.

*

The night of 9 December 1978, the day before my mum's twenty-seventh birthday, was cold enough that headlights shone off the ice on the roads. My parents were travelling down a dual carriageway in a taxi outside Winchester when it was hit by a car being driven in the wrong direction by a drunk man. The taxi flipped, landing on its roof, the metal as it slid firing sparks into the dark. Dad escaped with broken ribs and a head injury requiring stitches. Mum broke her jaw, and what was initially thought to be whiplash was later found to be a subluxation of the neck. An incomplete or partial dislocation. They'd been hit with such force it knocked her bones out of line.

Her mother, Thelma, claimed to have known that something bad had happened long before the phone rang with the news. She said it fell upon her as she was climbing into bed: a surety her daughter needed her. It lay across her chest so heavily she couldn't sleep. Mum was in hospital for weeks while Dad looked after Alison and Glenn (this was three years before I was born) at the naval married quarters where they were living near Portsmouth. She would emerge with her jawbone wired together, and for years afterwards it would stiffen when unused for any length of time. Sometimes she would need to stretch it, opening and closing her mouth as though in silent conversation with no one to bring a temporary end to a dull and taunting ache.

Back at their house that 5 November, the charred scent of fireworks was still hanging in the air. Dad sat in his armchair, grimacing slightly as he leant forwards to pick up the remote. When he did relax, it was by watching bad action films. He'd a particular, inexplicable fondness for *Passenger 57*, a 1992 film starring Wesley Snipes as a security consultant who foils a plot to free a captive terrorist during a commercial airline flight, and *US Marshals* from 1998, in which Tommy Lee Jones (who in a certain light Dad looked a lot like) has to track down a fugitive, again played by Wesley Snipes. Maybe it was because they were both films about strong, silent men who did their thing no matter what stood in their way and refused to explain themselves to anyone. Maybe he just really liked Wesley Snipes.

I waited for the advert break. When it was quiet, and I thought I might get his attention, the urge to crack his tough veneer finally overcame me. I asked what he remembered about the crash. He shrugged. It was dark, he said. Dark and cold and wet. He recalled the car coming towards them and thinking it was fast, and that was that.

'What do you mean *that was that*?' I said.

'That was that.'

'But what happened afterwards?'

'What do you mean *what happened afterwards*?'

'After the crash. What did you do?'

He was puzzled by why I might ask, or why he might do something so pointless as tell me.

'I pulled the door off and hit the driver and got your mother out. And that was that.'

'You pulled the door off and hit the driver and got Mum out?'

'Yes.'

'And that was that?'

I tried to imagine him in the rain on the road, pulling the door off the wreck of a car with his wife inside it. I wondered how terrified he must have been that she would die. Would he have survived without her? Would he have been able to go on? Who was he at that precise moment, standing at the end of everything and at the beginning of something else. These,

I suppose, were the things I was trying to get to. His story. Whatever lies in the shadows between the rocks.

He went into the kitchen and poured us each a large glass of whisky. This had never happened before. As the preamble to him finally revealing something deeper of himself, it felt a little on the nose, like something that might happen in the film we were watching. Dad smiled. I smiled. He threw the whisky down his throat and went to bed.

Mrs Bennett was right. When the former treasurer of the Saltwater Mansions management company, Leonard Curtis, quit the role a few years after Caroline's disappearance, he had indeed travelled to New Zealand for love. She was right too about the name; he had married a woman called Maggie. Leonard might not have had a social media presence – I had searched for him many times in the last few months – but his wife did. I found her tagged in a Facebook photograph in which she and a man, both in their seventies, pose for the camera in a Greek restaurant. They are standing close together and smiling, the burst of light from the flash bouncing back off their eyes. Just as I was beginning to panic about a fantasised scenario in which the search for Caroline was about to mean me flying to the other side of the world, I realised I recognised the restaurant, with its blotched ochre pillars and fake tumbling vines, as being one not too far away, one I'd visited. What Mrs Bennett hadn't known was that, having found love, Leonard Curtis had returned to the windswept Kent coast.

I immediately messaged Maggie, doing my best to explain that I thought the man she was with might be the Leonard Curtis formerly of Saltwater Mansions, and that I was interested in the mystery of Caroline Lane. He responded quickly, inviting me to his house to discuss the matter further. Caroline Lane, he said, was someone that he thought about a lot.

Leonard and Maggie lived at the very end of a wide, quiet street in a sleepy little village just a twenty-minute drive away. Only the distant sound of a hedge trimmer troubled the calm people retired to a place like this to enjoy. I parked the car and checked again that I had the right address, before I made my way up the steep stone steps to Leonard's front door. His house was higher than those of his neighbours, raised like an altar, as though this was the place to which the road had always led. They welcomed me in, and as I removed my trainers I was struck by the tidiness of their home: the straight row of well-shined shoes, the ornaments sitting equidistant on the mantel, sofa cushions resting square against the seat. Remnants, I assumed, of his military past.

Long since retired, Leonard and Maggie liked to wake up late and take long holidays. They spent a couple of months visiting family in America over Easter, and they'd do the same in Canada before the year was out. But most days, they said, were the same. They ate and watched TV and did the crossword. So it was nice to have new people to talk to. Especially about something that intrigued them as much as the mystery of Caroline Lane.

Making small talk before we got to the matter at hand, I asked Leonard what had brought him to Saltwater Mansions in the first place. It would be his pleasure to tell me all about it, he said, though I didn't understand then that the answer was tragedy, and am not sure I'd have asked if I had known.

Sometime in the spring of 1997, Leonard's first wife started to experience bouts of brain fog. Muddled thinking. Stumbled words. Difficulty co-ordinating her movements. Simple acts she'd always taken for granted, like climbing the stairs or putting the kettle on, suddenly presented complex challenges. A specialist diagnosed her with Parkinson's disease, which seemed at the time like the worst possible news. She made adjustments to her life to try and cope, but the episodes became more severe. Leonard had to help her slide her feet into her slippers, her arms into the sleeves of her coat, all these small acts of love you don't expect to undertake until much later on in life. The small things you do because love is small things.

When it seemed like her condition was worsening, they went back to see the specialist only to find he'd retired, and that his successor disagreed with the initial diagnosis. The new tests he ordered pointed towards something else: progressive supranuclear palsy, a neurodegenerative disease that quickly deteriorates then kills entirely specific volumes of the brain. The only other PSP sufferer Leonard had heard about was the comedian Dudley Moore, and the outcome was inevitable. The nervous system just collapses. Erases you piece by piece until you're gone. You love someone and then they disappear.

After his wife died, Leonard decided to use the life insurance money to buy a flat he could rent out. He liked a project, and in his grief he needed one, to distract himself if nothing else. It helped to have something to manage, something to wake up for in the morning, to take his mind off things. He wasn't expecting to buy the first place he saw, but there was something special about Saltwater Mansions, and about flat fifteen, the size and the feel and the footprint of it. Though it was a few floors above Caroline's, flat fifteen had a similarly sprawling layout: a large kitchen, a long corridor and a spacious lounge at the far end, with the added bonus of a balcony offering a fine view of the sea. It was an investment that all but guaranteed him security in retirement, it required minimal input, and he didn't need a specialist education to be a private landlord. He never thought this was how his life would turn out. But death had done what death does. It had picked him up and put him somewhere else.

The early 2000s saw an abundance of empty properties appear in Margate. Since the tourist economy collapsed there were hundreds of unsold holiday homes, abandoned B & Bs and entire spare floors in defunct hotels. It was a matter of take your pick. Unlike the locals concerned about the death of the town, or the businesses that needed customers through the doors, Margate's decline was welcomed by London's local authorities. They had a problem: what to do with destitute people. Unpalatable though it may have been to admit, London's destitute, many of them homeless, poor, vulnerable, addicts, children in care or ex-offenders, were considered a burden on resources. Central government had repeatedly slashed council budgets. Housing benefits were capped. Social services were overrun. They needed a solution and were behoved to think big.

The answer they arrived at was to encourage these people to move to Margate. Little thought, if any, was given to the notion they may have their only friends and family in the city. Or that, in some cases, these connections to their communities, and their stories, could be fundamental to their well-being. Though they themselves may have been wary of losing these connections, the vulnerable people, who in some cases didn't have a roof over their heads at all, understandably struggled to say no to the offer of a new home with a lovely sea view.

But with Margate's own local council budgets being cut and its tourist economy in free fall, the town didn't have the money or infrastructure needed to cater for the newcomers. Especially when their number was further bolstered by the arrival of refugees. They too had been sent to the coast by London boroughs that couldn't find the space or bear the cost of allowing them to settle. By 1999, police estimated there were more than 1,500 refugees living in Cliftonville, the ladder of little roads that linked Margate's east side to the shore. The majority were from Kosovo, Kurdistan, Albania and Afghanistan, escaping conflict, persecution and in the case of the Afghanis the fundamentalist rule of the Taliban.

Housing refugees in their community caused consternation among some of the locals, who blamed them for an increase in public order offences, littering, indecency and knife crime. Some nicknamed Cliftonville 'Kosoville'. Local tensions over immigration were seized upon by populist politicians, who exploited the situation to build support for parties like UKIP, the UK Independence Party. Their leader, Nigel Farage, stood to become MP for South Thanet years later in 2015. He failed, but with a sizeable 32 per cent of the vote. A year later, Thanet would elect to leave the European Union by a majority of almost two to one, despite warnings of a negative impact that would be felt more keenly in poor coastal areas than elsewhere in the country.

Under the weight of these two concurrent influxes, our vulnerable underclass and another country's huddled masses, not to mention the government's unwillingness to fund or create change, Margate couldn't cope. House prices bottomed out. Crime spiked. Money vanished. Politicians were nowhere to be seen and bins spilled their guts across the streets. The landscape might have been primed for the arrival of the artists, but living in Margate around the turn of the century was hard for everyone. The town was as unforgiving as it was forgotten. Life here simply went on.

*

Wherever he found himself, it was in Leonard's nature, and his training, to bring order to chaos. While most considered the business of the Saltwater Mansions management company too tedious to endure, Leonard embraced it, even though he was only a landlord and didn't live there himself. Numbers, mathematics and solving problems were his thing, so he volunteered for the position of treasurer. He got a kick from knowing what money was coming in and going out, then using that knowledge to see where funds could be saved for the benefit of the residents. It felt good to be able to use his skills again, now that military life was in his past. The only real drawback to being treasurer was dealing with a certain Caroline Lane.

When Leonard turned up to the 2006 AGM, he encountered a man he didn't know. He was smartly dressed and polite enough. In fact he was almost apologetic. It took Leonard a little while and a few enquiries among the other attendees to figure out exactly who the man was, but gradually the facts of the matter revealed themselves in a most unexpected way. Caroline had brought her father along.

As Caroline's father wasn't a leaseholder, and management company rules stated that only leaseholders could attend AGMs, Leonard asked if he'd kindly leave. Had Caroline informed them beforehand that she intended to bring her father to a leaseholders' meeting, which Leonard thought was awkward and a bloody odd thing for a woman of her age to be doing anyway, he'd probably have allowed it. But the way he saw things, Caroline was always fighting against him trying to get his work done, and he'd had enough. He was going to stick to the rules.

They argued for a while, and when she insisted her father stay, Leonard cancelled the meeting altogether. He'd rather have the burden of organising another AGM than break with protocol on nothing so much as a whim. Especially not for her. He found Caroline too unhelpful and difficult. Maybe she was in a stressful job, as she liked to remind people was the case, but that didn't mean she shouldn't play nice. As Leonard understood it, Caroline just wouldn't come down to their level. Add to that her cantankerousness, her refusal to accept that what anyone else was saying was true, her sheer bloody-mindedness, and his willingness to bend became non-existent. He showed her and her father to the door.

In the years that followed the 2009 AGM, when Leonard was pushing invoices through Caroline's door with an increasing sense of both urgency and futility, he never truly believed she might be dead, even when that seemed to be the consensus at which the other neighbours were beginning to arrive. To him it was more likely she'd had a breakdown. Maybe she wasn't there because she'd been institutionalised. She'd always seemed troubled, after all. Her erratic behaviour in the AGM and bringing her father to a leaseholders-only meeting were just two examples of many.

We moved through to the dining room, where the tablecloth was pressed as crisply as the sheet on an army bed.

'What about you?' Leonard asked. 'What do you think?' I explained that while I was intrigued by what happened to Caroline, and also assumed she was dead, I was more interested in what it might be possible for me to figure out: who she'd been when she was there. While I didn't acknowledge as much, a part of me had been waiting for an opportunity to present my multiverse of Caroline Lanes to someone as interested in the subject as I was.

'There's lots of possible versions of her,' I said. In one, the urgently dyed hair made her a fugitive from the law. In another, the gothic candlelit four-poster bed made her a high-end dominatrix. In another, she was a spy. Like Mrs Bennett, Leonard recalled Caroline claiming to have worked in government.

'I've a vague memory of her mentioning a job at the Italian embassy,' he said. 'But if you asked her anything about it she'd just go quiet. She was always reluctant to offer up any more details than that.' I did my best to bolster the theory with further evidence. It didn't mean she was a spook, but she was certainly fluent in other languages. Her shelves heaved with foreign-language books. On the matter of her lack of personal correspondence, spies, it seemed safe to presume, were reticent to hand out their addresses, and so weren't much of a burden on the postman come Christmas time. The British Airways air hostess uniform hanging in her wardrobe did little to dispel the notion either, even if it relied on a somewhat outmoded understanding of modern spycraft, as though it were something more accurately depicted in the 1960s espionage television series *The Avengers* than the books of John le Carré. And judging by the video which showed that her last act in flat nine might have been to dye her hair in a hurry, it could be argued with some conviction she needed a disguise. What better explanation for the fact that Caroline hasn't been found than that she didn't want to be?

If Caroline was a spy, I said, it might colour her response to someone like me trying to tell her story. Leonard didn't feel the same. Perhaps it was a symptom of his old age, he said, or of his experiences of life and love and pain and grief, but he thought she might like it. He considered himself quite a happy, laid-back guy. The way he saw it, if someone came to him and said, 'Leonard, you had a twenty-five-year army career and I'd like to hear about it,' he'd tell them everything they wanted to know.

'Because the hope is, when you retire and die and you get buried, you want your daughter or your grandson to look back on your life and say how good you were. If you've sat in your house your entire life and done nothing, they'll only be able to talk about you for five minutes. But if you have a story, and they know your story – because that's the thing, no one ever really asks – maybe, after you're gone, they can keep you alive. Maybe they can talk about you all day.'

Nine

Leonard was all too familiar with sitting in Mr Marjoram's office waiting to find out how much trouble he was in. It made him want to smoke. Mr Marjoram said the only thing that impressed him about Leonard was his determination to amount to nothing. Leonard lit a cigarette. That was his last day of school.

His mother, Elaine, wasn't much pleased by the situation and liked to wake Leonard early each morning to look for work. The problem was that every job Leonard got lasted less than a day. He'd been a builder, a welder, a carpenter, and now he was running out of trades to try. Desperate to find something that might stick, Elaine told him: 'You have to apply yourself, to turn up every day, even if it's to a lost cause.' There was something he did like to apply himself to, but it was an answer she wouldn't like. He said it anyway. Meeting girls.

Leonard's best friends, Harry, Colin and Briggs, would be overcome by terrible nerves at the dances. They stood at the sides with their backs to the wall as if all the women were doused in horse shit, and the women responded in kind. But Leonard moved around the room with a confidence that belied his sixteen years. He knew exactly who he was and people were drawn to it. More often than not, if he wanted to talk to a girl she would want to talk to him. His stepdad joked that if Leonard had been half as good at learning as he was talking to girls, they'd have an Einstein on their hands. Maybe then he'd be able to keep a job.

It was on Brighton beach one hot, cloudless Sunday afternoon that Leonard met Wendy. She was sitting on the pebbles with her friends. He was walking by and caught her looking. He smiled. She smiled back. He stubbed out his cigarette and went to say hello. Harry, Colin and Briggs couldn't believe what they were seeing. They all agreed Leonard was a lucky bastard. Wendy had long legs and beautiful round eyes. Leonard sat on the pebbles beside her until eventually the numbness in his arse made its way down to his ankles. He wasn't sure he'd ever be able to stand up again but it seemed like a price worth paying. It was rare to see Leonard and Wendy apart after that.

One night in a pub a few months later, Leonard met Wendy's ex-boyfriend, Frank. Everyone in town knew who Frank was. He was big and muscular, with a stare that could flay a side of beef. Any other new boyfriend of Wendy's he'd have torn apart. But not Leonard. Nobody could explain why, but Frank grew fond of Leonard, and any time they ran into one another he'd drop what he was doing to shake Leonard's hand, sometimes so vigorously it felt like he might pump his arm from its socket. Harry, Colin and Briggs would look on from a hiding place on the other side of the pub as if they were watching a schoolboy tame a lion.

Elaine reminded Leonard that being good with girls wouldn't get him a steady job. She urged him to look a little deeper than that; to find a passion he could convert into a skill.

'That's the recipe for happiness,' she said. 'Then you'll never work a day in your life.' Leonard wasn't really sure what she meant, but he saw how important it was to her and promised to give it some thought.

Besides girls, the only other thing that came to mind was drawing. Art lessons had been the one subject at school that held his attention. He could draw anything. No matter how technical – the more technical the better – an image would pass unencumbered from his eyes to his fingertips. He liked to draw things to figure out how they worked. When he drew something, it was as though he had X-ray vision. He could see the insides of it in operation: the cranks and cogs and chains, the wheels and the levers, all the individual moving parts that make the whole. He could take it apart and put it back together again.

One evening Leonard was on his way to pick Wendy up on his scooter when he ran into Frank. Frank was smiling. He didn't look like he was about to kill someone, and Leonard had never really seen him this way before.

'I just signed up to join the army,' Frank said. 'I'm going to be a draughtsman.'

Leonard didn't much believe in fate. He didn't much believe in anything. But he was struck by Frank's sense of purpose, the way it brightened his eyes and straightened his back. Leonard knew immediately that he wanted this same thing, to know he was going somewhere after all.

Within a week of passing the army entry exam, Leonard was offered a position as a driver-operator. Not that he fully understood what it meant. A few days after that he was sent 100 miles away for eighteen straight weeks of training. He said goodbye to Wendy and never saw her again.

Training was hard and continually being told what to do wasn't Leonard's idea of a good time. His bunkmates explained to him that, on this basis alone, he might have made a terrible decision when he joined the army. He'd have agreed were it not for the pay-off. For every hour he spent running around a field, doing press-ups or carrying one of the other recruits up a hill on his back, he'd spend another being taught about machines and engineering by people who knew what they were talking about. Trucks and cranes and tanks. Gigantic vehicles that could crush and lift and destroy. How to drive them. How to fix them. How to take them apart. How only one piece need be missing for the whole thing never to work again; what it takes to put something broken back together.

Leonard was in the barracks with the squaddies when the orders came down: they were being posted to Libya to build an airfield. While the others gathered their possessions, Leonard barely looked up from the sketch he was doing in his notebook. He wasn't part of the squadron so he wouldn't be going, and they ignored him like they always did until someone pointed out they'd need a driver-operator for the deployment, and that Leonard was the only one on site. Two days later they were all living together in a big tent in the middle of the desert. It was so hot their boots sweated. At night he dreamt of his mother.

Most of the time, when they were outside digging a trench for the runway, they worked together just fine. But in the downtime, when they played cards and drained cold beers, Leonard understood that the squaddies had forged their camaraderie over years. He'd less interest in trying to break into their circle than they had in inviting him into it. Instead he indulged his new hobby: scavenging for materials. Cogs. Levers. Any old clock parts he could find. There was plenty of junk lying around the place, in homes that had been abandoned in a hurry, or buildings blown up in some war or another. In the evenings, when the air was cooler, he huddled over his bedside table and painstakingly cleaned, arranged and lowered the pieces into position. It would take him three months, the same amount of time it took a squadron of men to make a functioning airstrip, but by the time their mission was complete Leonard had finished the watch. It was ornate and intricate, eccentric and unique, its dial big enough to cover his wrist and half of his hand. He had never been prouder of anything in his life.

When they saw the watch the squadron were as impressed. They'd become fond enough of Leonard – the curious outsider with the weird pastime – that they shared the lurch he felt in his stomach when the customs officer at the airport snatched the watch and began to inspect it closely. Was he going to confiscate it? He met Leonard's panicked eyes with a grin, slid the watch on to his wrist and paraded it around the room, then showed it to a colleague, who looked up at Leonard and grimaced. What laws had he broken? Was he a thief for taking a rusted spring he found in the sand? Could he go to prison? Would he ever get out? As the customs officer approached, Leonard got ready to run.

'This watch, is it yours?' Leonard didn't move. The squadron froze around him. The man held it to a light that glinted off the teeth of its cogs. 'Because if you made it, you are a genius,' he said, and waved them through.

Leonard was the toast of the flight home. They'd no way of knowing for sure, but were it not for his watch and the airport's horologist, maybe the contraband cigarettes they'd stashed into the false bottoms of grease cans wouldn't have passed so smoothly under the customs officer's nose.

It had been a year since Leonard last saw his friends from back home and he missed them, missed the ease with which they spoke about things, the in-jokes and stories from their childhoods. But he worried. They'd been in Brighton working their regular jobs, and he'd been in the Libyan desert building an airfield. Would they still have anything in common? His concerns vanished quickly. They went to the pub at lunchtime and left only when the landlord locked the doors. Nobody was sober enough afterwards to notice the frost, or the ice on the road half an inch thick. Nor were they steady enough on their feet when they saw the glowing shop window across the street to run towards it as quickly as they did. Behind the glass was a rotisserie: four glistening roast chickens rotating on a spit.

'Manna from heaven,' Leonard said. They bought one each and shared a bench that looked out on a cold, lightless sea. Sucking every last ounce of flesh from the bones, they thought of nothing. It had been a beautiful day.

The car was Harry's father's, but he said it was his own. When he couldn't figure out how to turn the heating up, Leonard, Colin and Briggs laughed as hard as they'd ever laughed. They were still laughing when the car hit a patch of black ice and slid, the steering wheel spinning through Harry's fingers until soon they were travelling sideways, not driving but gliding, not laughing but screaming, hitting the concrete post of a bus stop with a violence that lifted the car into the sky and then brought it down so hard on the road that the car was a new shape like the future was a new shape. Then it was silent, but in the air around it the violence still moved and was heard.

Briggs climbed out first. Then Colin. Briggs looked at Colin. He asked him if he was OK and Colin said yes. Somehow, it was true: there didn't seem to be a scratch on him. Colin asked Briggs if he was hurt and he said he didn't think so. Then he checked himself over and said no. By some miracle, no. The driver's side door was hanging off. Harry crawled out through the hole and he was OK too, he said. Dazed but OK. They were all dazed and in shock. They were all hot on a cold night.

Leonard pushed himself out of the car backwards using his legs, which were working just fine. He wrapped his fingers round the underside of the car above him and pulled himself to his feet. His arms were working fine too. And his hands. He turned to his friends and said he was OK. They were all OK. How lucky they'd been. Harry looked at Leonard's face. He smiled and offered him a cigarette. Leonard hadn't smoked since he joined the army. But this, the crash, the four of them being together, it felt like now was a good time. So he said yes please, right now he'd like to smoke. Harry put the cigarette in his mouth and lit it. His hands were trembling. Leonard tried to suck it but he couldn't because his jaw was hanging off and the tobacco was wet because his face was covered in blood.

A car slowed as it approached, lit up constellations of glass on the road. The driver got out and stared at the wreckage, then at the four men who'd emerged from it, as though he couldn't understand what they were. He looked at them like they were an apparition. At Leonard. He looked at Leonard for the longest time.

'You have to take our friend to hospital,' Harry said. The man was reluctant. He had his girlfriend in the car. They'd been to Brighton. It was late and he had work in the morning. Harry said it more forcefully the next time, moving towards the man, who then agreed. Leonard was struck by the way the man looked at him. It was the look of a man seeing something for the first time.

Briggs helped lower Leonard into the boot of the car. His legs dangled over the back. Colin told him not to worry about the mess he was making. The blood would wash out.

Leonard apologised for not sticking around to help flip the car back on to its wheels so they could drive home. He said that and they nodded and said OK Leonard. Then the man drove him away with his eyes on the mirror, not the road.

From what Leonard could see through the blood, the nurse had white-blonde hair and was nodding at what the doctor was saying, that this hospital couldn't handle injuries like these, they didn't have the resources or the experience to meet his needs. Leonard suspected the fact he had needs at all was bad news, but he stayed calm. Maybe that was the cigarette. Hard to know. This was all happening to someone else. It was somebody else on this gurney being wheeled down a corridor, the sound of doctors running and the strip lights zipping by.

'Where am I going!?' he said, tugging at the leathers that strapped him to the bed. But the words didn't sound like that at all.

Leonard had heard of Queen Victoria Hospital in East Grinstead. It was an institution with a reputation among military types. This was where the pioneering plastic surgeon Archibald McIndoe treated shot-down fighter pilots during the Second World War. McIndoe had specialised in deep burns and serious facial disfigurements. He had been so good at his work that his staff called him the maestro and he called the patients his boys. There could be no doubt in Leonard's mind, after he arrived with his face held together by bandages, that he was now one of McIndoe's boys too.

Days passed before he woke up. When he did he saw the man in the next bed had deep-brown skin. A deeper, different brown than he'd seen skin before. Not brown like the skin of the nurses. Brown like cooked. That was what Leonard was thinking about when the doctor came and told him his eye didn't work any more. Then they left him for the night to get over it.

The nurses put up a Christmas tree with a little angel on the top and sang carols over the crying. One gave Leonard a present. He was thankful for the cobnuts, but he couldn't really eat them because he didn't really have a jaw, and he couldn't really thank them because he couldn't really speak.

Leonard was misshapen now. There was a dent as deep as an ashtray on the front left of his skull. The doctors said it was still impossible to know whether this affected his brain, but it certainly hadn't affected his ability to sketch. By drawing the contraption they built around his head, Leonard could think of it more as a feat of engineering – albeit one that made it impossible to sleep lying down, or for longer than an hour at a time – than the one thing keeping him from falling apart. The nurses liked Leonard's drawings and showed them to the other men on the ward. Everyone except for Clyde, who was down on the bed at the end and couldn't see.

Nobody knew much about Clyde. What Leonard did know he learnt from the night shift nurses when they thought everyone was asleep. Clyde was in his sixties and there had been an explosion that had seared off almost all of his corneas. Leonard couldn't imagine the grief of losing sight in both eyes. His own future would be different, certainly not the one he had planned for himself, but at least he would be able to see it. Clyde's was cast in darkness. Leonard would live without, but Clyde was trapped within.

Despite their situation, the other men on the ward liked to laugh and joke to pass the days. But for the first few months Leonard was in hospital, he didn't hear Clyde speak once. The only time he saw his face change much at all was when the radio broadcast news of an international crisis unfolding in Panama. Clyde couldn't hear it over Vincent's shouting about nothing in particular from bed number three.

'Can you keep it down?' Clyde asked.

'Don't you tell me to be quiet,' Vincent snapped back. Vincent was young and erratic. His fingers had been burnt off by a faulty gas heater and he was taking it badly.

Leonard lifted himself and his head brace out of bed, leant down to Clyde's ear and offered to read from the newspaper to him what a journalist had written about Panama. Apparently it could be the beginning of something. It didn't look good.

'Why would I want you to read to me?' Clyde said. His teeth were grey and his eyes were white. 'I'm not a fucking child!'

For the first four months of 1964, Leonard sat at Clyde's bedside most days and read the paper aloud, sometimes for hours, sometimes from front to back. When it seemed Clyde didn't care, he remembered what his mother had told him about turning up every day no matter what. But it was beginning to seem possible to Leonard that, with or without the accident, Clyde was just a grumpy old bastard.

When he told Clyde that The Beatles performed on the *Ed Sullivan Show* to a record television audience of 73 million, Clyde said their music was awful. When he told Clyde that Cassius Clay changed his name to Muhammad Ali weeks after becoming the heavyweight champion of the world, Clyde said who cares? When he told Clyde that the Great Train Robbers received prison sentences totalling 307 years, Clyde said what in God's name are you telling me this for? Leonard didn't really have much of an answer for that.

He didn't blame Clyde for being angry. Barely a week went by when he wasn't being whisked off to surgery for some operation or other, returning with his head bound entirely in bandages like the Invisible Man. The pain. The blackness. It was enough to drive anyone to the brink. It was certainly enough to make a man want Leonard to shut up.

The only time Clyde didn't seem to grumble was when Leonard read him the racing pages. Lists of horse names and racetracks, their odds and jockeys and form. A thin smile would appear on Clyde's face and stay there. It seemed to transport him somewhere else. Outside the dark of his body, to a garden in his mind.

It was the first warm enough day of the year when the two men sat on a bench out at the front of the hospital. Clyde smoked Woodbines in a wheelchair. Leonard read the form guide. When he was finished with the day's races, he closed the paper and they stayed a while, listening to the birdsong. A nurse passed. The sight of the two of them made her smile. Nobody had got as close to Clyde as Leonard, but Clyde still looked like he might punch Leonard on the nose if only he knew where it was.

The future had been playing on Leonard's mind recently. Since he lost sight, his dreams were blank. He worried there was nothing ahead of him.

'What will I do?' he asked Clyde.

'What are you talking about now?'

'After here. Do you think the army will take me back?'

Clyde sucked the cigarette between his yellow fingertips. Smoke swirled in pirouettes round his head.

'Is that what you think the point of this is?' he said. Leonard didn't understand. 'You think your accident happening was the world's way of telling you what you can't do?'

'I suppose.'

'And why do you suppose?'

'I drive bulldozers.' Leonard stretched his arms out.

III

'They're hardly going to let me do that if I can't see from here to here.' His voice wavered. His problem was becoming more real as he articulated it. It had taken him years to figure out how he might make something of his life. Now he had nothing.

Clyde leant forwards in his seat, his bandaged eyes aimed past Leonard at the horizon or thereabouts.

'You're thinking of it all wrong,' he said. 'Your accident wasn't the world's way of telling you what you can't do. It was the world's way of showing you what you can. That's what the things that happen in a life are. You just don't realise it until they're in the past.'

Leonard nodded.

'Now I'll tell you what you can do. You can take me inside and let me fucking sleep.'

Leonard slowly began to recover. It was something of a miracle considering the mess the crash had made of his face. In the days and weeks before he was finally due to leave hospital, he allowed himself to imagine what life might be like from now on. His mother wasn't keen on the idea, but he hoped to be able to return to the forces. It was likely to be difficult. His superiors were unsympathetic. They didn't feel that a man with half his vision could make a full contribution to army life, and so they'd earmarked him for a grunt job, working the stores or maintaining the barracks, some lame dog task like that.

But Clyde's words played over and over in Leonard's head during the meeting he'd had with them about his return. And maybe it was those, or the determination he'd discovered through his convalescence, that propelled Leonard to fight his corner. While he might not have been an ideal candidate for swinging wrecking balls, he had more to offer than stacking shelves or painting the walls of the mess hall. There could be no doubting his talent as a draughtsman. You only need one eye to draw, and nobody in their ranks was better at drawing than him. They fell silent. He continued. Remember, he said, he was skilled with numbers too. He'd been studying double-entry bookkeeping during his recovery and had become so proficient that even the hospital manager had sought him out for advice with the accounts. He might only have been able to stare across that desk with one working eye, but he'd seen submission on their faces that day. They hadn't believed him recalcitrant. They'd believed him right.

The doctors told Leonard he was free to go home on a Friday. His mother bought him a lime-green jumper and a small suitcase for the occasion. He put everything he owned inside it: his notebook, some fine pencils and the watch. When it was packed, he asked the nurses if he might stay a day longer. They laughed, but when he told them why they agreed. The following day was the Grand National at Aintree, the biggest meet in the horse racing calendar, and he wanted to listen to it with Clyde.

For the entire month before, Leonard had been reading out the race results, and Clyde had been assessing the form. Grumpily demanding Leonard speed up or slow down or repeat the lot from the top, he'd picked his three favourite nags: Supersweet, Pappageno's Cottage and Team Spirit. This last one drew smirks from the men on the ward that Clyde had been heckling all year.

As the start of the race approached, Leonard wondered whether Clyde would be in any fit state to enjoy it. A few days earlier he'd had another operation on his eyes. The surgeons said this one was a last-ditch attempt to make sure what remained of his life would at least be lived in some comfort, rather than excruciating pain. Ever since then he'd been so heavily medicated that he hadn't even been able to shout at Vincent, which was his number-one way of passing the time.

Regardless, Leonard read the sports pages aloud all morning, hoping the excitement might rouse him somehow. He was delighted when it worked. The nurses helped Clyde to a sitting position in front of the radio they'd arranged at the foot of his bed. As the commentary team ran through the runners and riders a final time, and a kind doctor returned with Clyde's betting slip, Leonard turned the volume up loud.

Nobody much fancied Team Spirit for the win. Most felt that the horse was too small for a race as famously tough as the Grand National. But Clyde identified something in the animal that others hadn't seen. He was courageous and plucky. Undeterred by disaster. Unrelenting in his desire to try.

For the majority of the race it looked like there was only one winner. By the second lap, Peacetown had built a substantial lead. But, fifty yards from home, the Irish jockey Willie Robinson, a small man with steely eyes and a wide smile, pushed Team Spirit to win by half a length.

When the men who were able attempted to lift Clyde from his bed and parade him around the ward in celebration, he told them all to leave him alone. Leonard put his arms round the old man, half expecting the same, but it never came. He didn't know whether, through the drugs and the excitement of victory, Clyde would remember that this was their last day together, so he chose not to say goodbye. Of the two men, only one spoke.

'Nice jumper,' Clyde said, and Leonard walked out into a world he saw anew.

Ten

Being an ex-military man, Leonard was formal enough in his manner that it seemed to surprise him at first, and then to amuse him, to suddenly be sharing old memories of such a difficult episode in his past with a relative stranger. I got the impression he didn't have reason to talk about these matters much, if at all, these days. While he spoke, I considered his age (he was almost eighty, which he said seated him in God's waiting room) and how he'd told me they didn't get many visitors. I'd never have been so rude as to raise it, but I couldn't help wonder whether this would be the last time he would ever speak about what went on at the hospital sixty years ago, and I was touched he'd done this with me.

Afterwards, as we whiled away the rest of the afternoon swapping theories about why Caroline might have left Saltwater Mansions, Leonard's story only became more poignant. It was a reminder that a life could be upended at any moment. That in the beat of a heart, our fortunes can change completely.

What was it that happened to Caroline in the summer of 2009? Was it sudden or a long time coming? A twist of fate or the looming of an existential threat? While they weren't about to lead me to the truth, Leonard's recollections of their encounters were illuminating. They painted a picture of a person on the edge. Someone who took her father to meetings of the management company was likely insecure, worried, troubled, angry, scared, or some combination of all these things. Whoever she'd been, this version of Caroline was wound tight like kindling straw. An argument. A breakdown. A sacking. Being hidden. Being found. The cost of a repaired fire escape. An unwanted knock at the door. A figure from her past. A prospect in her future. The smallest spark could have set her aflame.

It was a Saturday morning and autumn was tumbling into winter when I received a voice note from my friend Ed. Ed was someone I'd talked to about Caroline on many occasions over the previous five months. Huge chunks of his valuable free time had been lost to me complaining that I couldn't find out more about the vanishing woman of Saltwater Mansions, that the government still refused to confirm or deny she had worked in Whitehall, and how, though I'd interviewed a number of people from the block, I'd not been able to track down anybody else, besides Mrs Bennett, who had lived there at the same time. Most days I could do nothing but moan to Ed that I wanted a lead to drop out of the sky and land in my lap. This was why, right now, he urgently wanted to talk.

He'd just driven past Saltwater Mansions. It was surrounded by police cars, fire engines and ambulances. Something big was going down. This building with which I'd become so familiar, a scene I now associated with a frustrating sense of inertia as much as the mystery that had drawn me there in the first place, was suddenly one of movement and chaos. I grabbed my keys and drove towards it as quickly as I could.

A policeman was taping off the road as I arrived. I parked the car and walked along the pavement as far as

I was permitted to go. Between Saltwater Mansions and the cliff's edge was a thin patch of grass where a small crowd of onlookers had gathered. A man with a muzzled dog watched through binoculars, craning his neck for a better view. His friend was sitting on a fold-up chair, the kind people used for fishing. As I sidled into the space behind them, they were explaining in hushed tones to an inquisitive woman with silver eyebrows what they believed was unfolding across the street. The police were trying to evict a man from his flat. It was someone well known locally, particularly to the law, though they probably used the name he was given at birth. Everyone around here called him Crazy Barry.

An eviction, though dramatic on its own terms, wasn't all that rare an event in Margate. Rents were rising and the cost of living had soared. Gentrification had brought a great deal of money and opportunity to the town but, by and large, only to those who already had some in the first place. Margate's poor might have noticed the area changing – the rainbow-coloured homeware shops and pop-up Korean lunch joints were difficult to avoid – but, in terms of their finances, it hadn't affected their lives in any useful or desirable sense. If times were hard before the DFLs came en mass, they were probably harder still now.

I remarked that there was an unusually large police presence for an eviction. The man in the fishing chair shrugged, as though the reason was obvious, when in fact I'm not sure it was at all. 'It's because he's wearing a suicide vest,' he said. 'Barry's saying he's going to blow the place to smithereens.'

We watched for a while as the stand-off developed. In reality nothing was happening, or at least not that we could see, but as lunchtime approached the crowd grew bigger and more tense. I tried calling Dee to get a sense of what this felt like inside the building, but there was no answer. In case she hadn't looked out of her window or been evacuated by the police, I sent her a message saying someone named Crazy Barry was threatening to nuke the street, signing off with the words 'hopefully it's nothing to worry about'.

It would be hours before a specialist police team finally managed to coax an exhausted-looking Barry from the building and arrest him. When they did they discovered his vest wasn't full of explosives after all. He had taped three tins of beans together, stuffed them inside his jacket and told the men who'd come to kick him out it was a bomb. I was sure there must have been more to Barry's story than this episode with the eviction and the beans. Who knew what turns his life must have taken to reach this point. But it was the beans that made the papers, of course.

If I learnt one thing about Caroline that afternoon, it was only what I noticed once Barry was gone. A charmed snake of ripped police tape was dancing on the breeze, and as I walked to my car I took the opportunity to peer through the windows of Caroline's flat. I did this whenever I used this road these days, but now something was different. The windows had been cleaned, and behind them, in her old lounge, were teetering stacks of cardboard boxes. All these years after Caroline Lane left Saltwater Mansions, someone new was moving in.

When the sale of a property is forced, the money made, once all debtors have been paid, sits in a secure government pot. By my crude estimations, because of Margate's rocketing house prices, Caroline had just over £100,000 waiting to be claimed. The only person who could claim the money from the sale of flat nine was either Caroline herself or a next of kin presenting her death certificate. Regardless of whether or not she was wealthy enough to pay the mortgage on a flat she didn't use for thirteen years, £100,000 felt like an amount it'd be difficult to ignore. If she was to hear about it, that is. The sale was a good reason to think that someone who knew Caroline might come forward. Money is a great motivator, after all.

I'd often thought about what it might be like to meet a relative of Caroline's. There was a chance they would be willing to tell me about her. The fact that they were around to know her story would put to bed my anxieties about it vanishing with her, and I might finally be able to shake myself free of what my wife now joked was an obsession.

On the other hand, given that nobody had ever come looking for her at Saltwater Mansions, it was likely they were estranged. In reality, they might not know that much about Caroline, certainly not as she was in later life. Either way, I would probably have the grim task of informing them of what I had discovered – the post, the meeting, the state in which the flat was left – and what I thought it was all likely to mean: that Caroline was dead. I'd be visiting tremendous pain on them, regardless of whether they were still in touch. Out of cowardice more than kindness, this was something I didn't want to do. Still, I couldn't quite let go of the idea that there was something that might provide vital information about Caroline concealed somewhere in her flat, and that this may lead me to someone who knew her better. It was the only avenue I had left to explore.

When I texted Dee to ask if she knew who'd bought Caroline's old place, she said they were a young couple who'd recently got married. From their one brief meeting on the stairs, they struck her as nice and approachable, certainly enough that they might be willing to speak to me. It felt more than ever that the truth lay tantalisingly within reach, even if the idea that Caroline might have left a clue to her disappearance beneath the floorboards was more like something out of an Agatha Christie novel than a real missing person case. 'A woman I think is dead might have left a clue beneath your floorboards' would be an awkward opening gambit to make to the young couple who'd just moved into her flat. My best hope was to write them a letter and slip it under their door.

'No,' Lou said forcefully when she caught me hunched over my notebook at the dining table. 'You need to wait. Let them settle in. They might have literally just got married. They might still be in the honeymoon period, when everything is nice. Nothing is going to ruin that faster than someone asking whether you found a lady's head or whatever hidden in a jar in the wall cavity of your new home.' She had a point. I promised to give them a couple of weeks.

When I thought of our wedding, a few years before in 2019, it's not the time after it that sprang to mind. We'd not been able to afford much, so our honeymoon was one night in a hotel on Margate seafront, a fifteen-minute walk from our house. Shortly after checking out, our lives were quickly swallowed up by the hard work of parenting and trying to get by. Soon there was an extent to which it felt like the ceremony never happened, as though it had all been an especially lovely dream.

Dad wrapped ribbons round the bonnet of his car to drive Lou to the registry office and promised he knew where he was going. A little later, Lou texted me from the back seat. She wanted to let me know she was going to be late for our wedding because my father refused to look at a map. I said not to worry. He always finds a way. That's kind of what he does; just keeps moving forwards until the job gets done. When they arrived she was pale and he was smiling.

We were married with only our parents present. Mum cried. Dad shook my hand. I couldn't remember the last time we touched.

That afternoon we held a mock wedding ceremony in a pub for our family and friends. It was a Wednesday in June, because the hire was cheaper. We decorated the room ourselves and put a huge home-made cardboard sign on the wall that read 'Inconvenient Wedding Of The Year'. We probably didn't take it seriously enough. Maybe we'd do it differently now. You never know that about something until it's over: a wedding, a conversation, a life.

We walked up the aisle to Aretha Franklin's version of Sam Cooke's 'You Send Me', and walked back down to 'Life's a Happy Song' from *The Muppets* because our kids liked it. In my vows I spoke about how brave she was. A few days before she'd called her boss out for being a bully. It was a scene I imagined as being like something from a film. She said she loved me even though my head was too big for my body. When we kissed, the whole room burst into applause.

Later, as I reached the part of my speech where I thanked my parents for the years of love they'd shown me and the sacrifices they'd made, Dad loudly asked why I was still speaking. Everybody laughed. It was funnier than anything I'd said all afternoon. But nobody knew what I knew. It wasn't just a joke. It was a deflection, a public display of his belief that his story wasn't worth being told.

Somebody once said to me that the day of my wedding would be so overwhelming it would be hard to take it all in. That it's a good idea to pause, now and then, if you can. Halfway through the afternoon I found a quiet spot round the back where I could be alone for a while. The pub sat on the River Stour. Kayakers paddled past smiling wedding guests smoking cigars in the sun on the veranda. A breeze carried songs to the bottom of the garden, where a family of pigs lived in a pen full of oily black mud.

I could see Dad down there with my eighteen-month-old son. They were laughing and waving at the boats cruising by. It seemed quite possible they'd been doing it for hours. Dad lifted him on to his lap. There's a photograph of them in this moment. A craggy hand saddling the soft hump of infant belly, their whole world there in the cradle of each other. I watched Dad wait for his breath as it slipped in and out of his grasp.

When we got into bed that night I told Lou I thought Dad didn't seem right. There was something different about him I couldn't quite define. An outline smudged that had once been crisp. A shallowing of what was deep. A distance where he'd once been near. All those things I'd never asked him, that he had never said.

Eleven

Ever since one of their soon-to-be neighbours told them the story of Caroline and how she'd disappeared on an otherwise ordinary morning thirteen years before, Beth hadn't been able to get it out of her mind. While waiting for her purchase of flat nine to complete, she spent entire days attempting to piece together Caroline's family tree. The reasons for her fascination were two-pronged. As well as the intrigue everybody in Saltwater Mansions appeared to share, Beth hoped that, if she could understand who Caroline was, maybe she could dispel her niggling fear that living in the flat where a woman disappeared might be too spooky to bear. It was for this reason that she was excited to hear what I knew about Caroline, and happy to show me around the place where the subject of our mutual obsession once vanished into thin air.

Beth apologised for the mess. She and her partner Jon knew there would be lots of work to do when they moved in, but they grossly underestimated exactly how much. After sitting empty for so long, Caroline's old home had fallen into a state of considerable disrepair. There was damp on the sills. Leaks between the panes of double glazing. Rotten kitchen wood and slipping bathroom tiles. Not one room had escaped the need for urgent attention, but buying the flat had burnt through all their resources. Now Beth and Jon were out of cash.

With no real experience of decorating, even less so renovations, they had no choice but to attempt the work themselves. Armed with nothing more than YouTube tutorials, and emboldened by being young and in love, they descended beneath the floorboards and completely rewired the electrics. Managing to do it without getting electrocuted was a source of some pride, but plumbing, they were quick to discover, was a different beast entirely. It'd be a while yet before they could do their washing up anywhere other than the bathtub.

Slow though it may have been, chronicling the flat's renovation on Instagram helped Beth to remember how far they'd come. The first room, where Caroline had a gothic four-poster bed, ornate candle holders and little else, was full of flight cases now. Jon was a touring musician. One day it would be his studio, but they hadn't started on that yet. So the second room, the lounge, was the first to be completed. Its walls were lined with brightly coloured prints by local artists, many of whom had become friends. A fluorescent orange poster from an amateur dramatics production of *Little Red Riding Hood* reminded Beth of her childhood, and a huge TV was held partially responsible for the stuttering pace of the work so far.

Watching the footage from when the Saltwater Mansions management company first entered Caroline's flat in January 2022, it wasn't the kitchen with plates in the sink and vests on the clothes horse that most stuck in my memory. Nor was it the bedroom with the stowed mosquito net, where you could still make out the shape of her body in the sheets. Though Dee only briefly poked her camera through the door before moving on, as though it were too desolate a sight to behold, the room I remembered most was this third room. On the day Caroline left there was a large, round wooden table here, with four chairs tucked beneath it, and bare walls that made the space seem eerily liminal. It reminded me of the dining room on a shipwreck.

Today, the third room was home to rails upon rails of vintage clothing. Beth was particular in her tastes. Her second-hand clothes shop in Margate Old Town outlasted many of those that sprung up around it through the first years of gentrification, when it seemed DFLs with dreams of being business owners were opening and closing shops every other week. This could be put down to curation. Her customers knew they were buying quality. She'd built for herself that most valuable but elusive of things: a good reputation. It was so good that she didn't need the shop any more and could work from this room, taking orders online and shipping them out from the comfort of her own home.

Beth's reputation is what led to her receiving a call from Janet, one of the current directors of the Saltwater Mansions management company, in January 2022. She and the other members were in the process of emptying one of the flats in the building. Something about the owner seeming to evaporate and a forced sale signed off by a judge. They had entire closets full of vintage clothing to get rid of, and no idea what to do with it all. What they wanted to know was, could Beth help?

It wasn't unusual for Beth to be invited to a house clearance, but it was unusual for her to be interested. House clearances tended to involve clothes that weren't right for her customers: the clothes of old, dead people, musty-smelling suits and dresses moth-eaten beyond repair. Janet, however, had caught her at an opportune moment. It was January, typically a quiet month for small seaside businesses, and she had a little money for stock left over from the Christmas gift rush. Figuring there was nothing to lose, she headed to Saltwater Mansions with low expectations and an empty suitcase in the boot of her car.

Her first impressions were that whoever had lived in flat nine was well-read. There were books everywhere, many of them haphazardly piled on interesting furniture that looked as if it might have been shipped over specially from abroad. These, though, were not her concern. She made a beeline for the wardrobe: a collection of fabulous knits, Laura Ashley dresses and trench coats, all size eight to ten. Whoever owned them had been well dressed at some point in the past. Beth couldn't stop grinning. Almost everything she saw would be snapped up by her customers. She'd struck oil in her own backyard.

Before long, though, it became difficult to concentrate. The clothes might have been beautiful, but so was the flat. It was big and light, unusual and perfectly appointed. When she overheard someone from the management company talking about how it had been empty for thirteen years and was soon to be on the market, her heart rattled. She knew immediately. She wanted it.

Beth hated the flat where she lived. Just a ten-minute walk inland, on the other side of Cliftonville, it had belonged to her mother, Rosa. They'd lived there together for eight years until Rosa's death in the summer of 2020. After that, the flat became Beth's. Home ownership had exposed her to a set of issues she'd only been distantly aware of before, when Rosa took care of everything to do with their living situation. Now she was part of a resident-led building management company, not dissimilar in function or disfunction to the one that ran Saltwater Mansions, and their interactions were the stuff of nightmares. Without exaggeration, her neighbours were some of the most awful people she'd ever had the misfortune to meet.

No matter how small the issue: a creaking fire escape door, the sharp scent of cat piss on the communal stairs, the loud arguments round the clock from flat three, they disagreed over everything. They sent her nasty emails and moaned at her by the post-box. Every interaction they had seemed designed to gradually erode the sense of community she'd been needing, in her grief, to find on her doorstep. Soon she was sneaking out through the fire exit most days in the hope that she wouldn't see them, and the rest of the time locking herself in her flat like a recluse. Added to the pain of losing her mother, the stress of dealing with these people meant Beth had a sort of breakdown. Some mornings she woke up and wondered if she'd been crying all night.

Back in flat nine, Beth sneakily took photographs of as many different rooms as she could to show her fiancé Jon where they were going to live one day (she instinctively knew he'd fall in love with it too). Then she told Janet that she'd love to buy not just a few frocks, but the whole bloody place. She didn't actually have the money. She'd have to figure out the business of it all later. But she didn't need to tell them that. Not yet.

Barely a day went by in the next six weeks when Beth didn't refresh the estate agent's website with an impatience that began to border on mania. Eventually, it appeared. For sale: flat nine, Saltwater Mansions. But Margate in 2022 was a highly competitive market for anyone wanting to buy property. Sellers could line up a dozen viewings in a day, and buyers could reasonably fear getting gazumped at the last minute by a cash-rich second home owner.

This was the third wave of gentrification. Margate had become popular and expensive. There was no shortage of monied types wanting to live there, many of whom would table higher bids than Beth could ever afford. Luckily, from her own experience being part of a management company, she knew that the other homeowners in the building would have a say over which applicant was successful. She also knew the likelihood of the other buyers being buy-to-let landlords, the type of people who'd been snapping up Cliftonville property these last few years and letting it out to private tenants at exorbitant prices. A couple down the road had just purchased the block next to their house and kicked out the old lady who lived in the basement flat so that they could renovate and re-let it at a far higher monthly rate, much to the chagrin of the neighbours who'd been on this street their whole lives. There was a real danger that anyone wanting to buy flat nine might also be meaning to flip it for profit, or to list it on Airbnb, so they could sit back and soak up the passive income, undermining any sense of community in the block.

All of these options shut the locals out of the housing market in their own town, locals like Beth and her friends. It was an ugly symptom of gentrification, and she definitely wasn't a part of it. She wanted to make flat nine a home. Somewhere she could stay forever. Somewhere she might start a family one day. So she didn't just place a bid. She made a plea. In granting her permission to buy Caroline's old flat, the residents wouldn't just be getting a new name on the buzzer by the front door. They'd be getting a neighbour, where for almost a decade and a half there'd been none. Not that this was a fact they needed reminding of. It was all any of them seemed to talk about.

Because of tedious complications that arose from the sale being forced, it would be many, many months before Beth was finally handed the keys to Saltwater Mansions. She passed the time until then dreaming of her exit from her current arrangement and making plans for how she might decorate flat nine. Most of her days off were spent in Margate Library, tracking down old photographs of the building and studying its heritage. She wanted to honour its history, and as time went on she wondered if she might also be able to honour its previous occupant, the mysterious Caroline Lane.

Beth hoped that something had fallen through the gaps between the floorboards. A letter maybe. A page from a diary. A photograph of a tender moment with her handwriting on the back. That she would find it when she was under there re-wiring the electrics. Maybe she could frame it and hang it on the wall. In the end there was nothing, but Beth's fascination with the disappearing woman didn't wane when she moved in. If anything, she started to feel even closer to this person she didn't know, as though a part of Caroline was still there, even if it wasn't something she could hold.

Caroline hadn't been much younger than Beth's mother, Rosa, when she was last seen. Beth could tell from the clothes she left behind that, like Rosa, Caroline had been elegant and vivacious, independent and spirited. She wasn't sure if she believed in fate or the presence of spirits or anything like that, but on the day she first went to Saltwater Mansions to look through Caroline's wardrobe, she'd been wearing a bracelet her mother bought for her round her wrist. The bracelet had a little silver baby dangling from it that fell off and skittered across the floor. Beth picked it up and wondered if this was a sign from her mother that one day she'd walk around this room, holding a daughter of her own.

After Beth finished showing me around her flat, we sat down in the lounge to drink coffee and trade theories about Caroline. She didn't believe that Caroline's behaviour at the 2009

AGM necessarily meant she was obstinate or aggressive. Beth had been in such meetings. She had been surrounded by men who would patronise and belittle her, men who wouldn't take her seriously or listen to what she had to say. She knew all too well the slow-crushing anxiety of sitting in somebody else's flat with a group of near-strangers who didn't value her opinions. She'd felt what it's like to not be considered equal, the bite of loneliness in a busy room.

What if Caroline wasn't being difficult? What if she was in fact simply fighting for her rights as a homeowner? Caroline hadn't asked for anything in that AGM that she wasn't legally or even morally entitled to. While it may have been finicky, it made sense that the Saltwater Mansions accounts be audited by an independent third party. It might have been annoying, but it remained reasonable, maybe even sensible, to question the quote Leonard Curtis secured for the repair of the fire escape, given that he'd obtained it from an acquaintance. That's just called doing your due diligence, isn't it? She believed his motives were good, but the world wasn't short of people on the make. It was better to be sure.

If Caroline wasn't convinced that anybody else at the AGM would make a good secretary for the management company, Beth had nothing but sympathy. Since her mother died she'd sat in drab living rooms full of her neighbours on lots of occasions, and she wouldn't trust most of them to walk her dog, let alone run the business of the block with her money. Just because she shared walls and floors and ceilings with another person, it didn't mean they'd earned her trust. Beth was an optimist, but being an optimist didn't make everyone nice.

Looked at from one angle, Caroline was petty and combative. Looked at from another, she was simply standing up for herself. Beth doubted that the minutes would have reflected so badly on a man who'd behaved the same way. In a man this kind of behaviour was strength, in a woman it was stubbornness. In a man determination, in a woman resistance. Perhaps, Beth felt, the question that arose was not what was wrong with Caroline in the days before her disappearance, but whether we can ever really tell the stories of those who aren't around to tell them themselves.

Beth's dog was asleep on a cushion. A light snore fluttered on his lips. As Beth and I talked, I imagined Caroline returning from the kitchen with a glass of wine. Reclining on the sofa to watch a film. Sighing when someone knocked on the door, gripped by indecision over whether to answer. I wondered how she'd feel about the lounge being full of someone else's things, or that a life would one day flourish where hers, not long later, seemed to stop.

Beth opened a plastic crate. Inside it were some of her mother Rosa's most treasured possessions. She took out a collection of notebooks bound together by a gnarled length of string and stroked them tenderly as we talked. These were the diaries Rosa kept on and off for her entire life, and this was just a small selection of them. There were more in the bedroom. Beth wanted to go through them, but she hadn't found the emotional strength quite yet.

'Actually,' she corrected herself, 'that's a lie. I did look at one, but the first words I read were about Mum having sex, so I decided to leave it for another day.' We talked more about her mother, about the complexities of grief, how it can consume you to the degree that you almost become it, or forget it's there. Maybe that's how we survive it, Beth said, and I agreed.

It was soon time for me to leave. I'd stayed much longer than I'd intended. I needed to collect my children from school, and the traffic was usually terrible at this time of day.

I offered to wash up the mug I'd been drinking from to save Beth the bother, but she refused because I'd have to use the bathtub. I couldn't really argue with her reasoning. As she showed me to the door, she suggested I could look at her mother's diaries if I wanted to. Not right now, but one day. It gave her comfort to know that Rosa had recorded her whole life story because she didn't want her mother to be forgotten. She thought it important, that it was kept, that it was told.

Twelve

Clive worked for Ford Motors. If asked, he'd say he was a simple engineer. In reality they had him flying between plants in Dagenham, Cork and Cologne on important business so regularly he often forgot what country he was having breakfast in. When Sandra went into labour with their first daughter in the spring of 1966, Clive had to rush for a plane to get back to Ilford. He only just made it in time.

Rosa was three and already had two siblings when Sandra and Clive first found her struggling to breathe. They didn't know a thing about genetics until a doctor called them into his office and explained that they both carried mutations in their genes. Their problem was with the CFTR (cystic fibrosis transmembrane conductance regulator) protein. Though her brother and sister were unaffected, Rosa had inherited cystic fibrosis, which mostly damages the lungs, but also the pancreas, liver, kidneys and intestines. Thanks to bad luck and vicious coincidence, she would require regular medical treatment her entire life. It would be useful, he said, to consider Brompton Hospital something of a second home from now on.

For those first few years they coddled her, never able to escape the feeling that they were preparing themselves for her death. Slowly though, as she became a lively, uninhibited child who enjoyed chasing her siblings around the garden, they realised that she deserved an existence so much fuller than this. So they promised themselves that Rosa would not grow up to feel any different from their other kids. They would let her out into the world and protect her freedom with everything they had.

Neither Clive nor Sandra had ever played an instrument in their life, so they couldn't quite figure out how all three of their children had such a startling gift for music. Alan played a superb French horn, and Gloria the piano like a natural. But when Rosa sang she revealed herself to have a prodigious talent. Nobody could believe that a voice like hers could come from the mouth of such a small child, especially one whose lungs didn't function in the way they were meant to. It was fragile yet powerful, angelic yet rich, and she had a mastery of its range that belied her tender age. One day, when Sandra took Rosa to the market and Rosa sang to herself while they shopped, a stranger told Sandra that Rosa's voice might be the most beautiful sound she had ever heard.

Though Clive and Sandra vowed never to tell Rosa what she could or couldn't do, by the time she was sixteen they realised she probably wouldn't have listened to them anyway. Her ears rattled with the piercings they'd rather she didn't get, and her scarlet lips and studded leather jacket reminded the horrified neighbours of Madonna. They drew their blinds when Rosa walked up the path, as though the mere sight of her was a threat to the sanctity of the neighbourhood. The truth was that they had nothing to worry about. Rosa wanted to leave as much as they wanted her to go. Her ambitions had outgrown Ilford. She yearned for drama and romance, for the spooked heartbeat of the city.

*

As they were entering the final year at the Royal Academy of Music, there wasn't a single one of Rosa's classmates studying opera who doubted the magic in her voice, or that she would one day be a star. The other girls dreaded the day when they'd walk into an audition room to find Rosa warming up. She might be putting them out of work for years to come.

Rosa didn't care much for being admired. What she wanted was to be a part of something, and when she was on that stage with the other students she didn't feel like an outsider any more. They may have been a ragtag bunch of wannabes from all kinds of different cultures and backgrounds, but they had a matter of great importance in common. They were all running away from something. There was Colette, a closeted Manhattanite who'd moved to London to escape her devout Catholic parents. There was Graham, a broke Glaswegian who didn't want to join the family scaffolding firm but had told them he was working down south as a builder. There was Romilly, a brilliant soprano and raging alcoholic. And here was Rosa, fleeing her mortality, finally feeling she belonged.

Every sixth Thursday, Rosa had an appointment at Brompton Hospital that made her late for class. The doctors were delighted by her progress. Over the last couple of years she'd suffered fewer infections. That reduced the need for invasive treatment. She wasn't cured and never would be, but she was experiencing something of a purple patch. Things were good. Nobody could pinpoint a reason for the upturn until a consultant she'd grown fond of suggested all the opera training might be helping to improve the condition of her lungs. They were a muscle, after all. What better workout than Puccini's 'O mio babbino caro'? He joked that Rosa might be the first person in the world to keep cystic fibrosis at bay using arias.

She left hospital that day believing she couldn't be happier. Then she received a call.

The Phantom of the Opera had only opened at Her Majesty's Theatre in London a year earlier, but Rosa had already forgotten how many times she'd been to see it. She identified just as much with the Phantom, a physically impaired outsider obsessed by music, as she did with Christine, the pure-hearted young woman with the seraphic voice he falls in love with. But more than that, she adored the tragic romance of it all. Appearing on that stage seeped into her dreams.

When Sarah Brightman left to open *Phantom* on Broadway, Rosa thought the phone call asking to see her for the part of Christine was a cruel practical joke. Perhaps one of her student colleagues had finally let their envy get the better of them. Why would *Phantom* be interested in her? She hadn't even graduated. She was twenty-one. She was from Ilford. She was sick. There was no way she could play Christine Daaé.

The first audition was a disaster. She'd expected to feel nervous, but her hands shook and her lips got dry and she could barely remember her own name. Afterwards she recalled nothing but anxiously retching into a plant pot and the vaguely furious expression on the face of the pianist, wondering why she was wasting his time. That night, her friends assured her these things are never as bad as they seem. They promised she'd feel better in the morning. But Rosa didn't believe them. She spent the next few days wandering aimlessly around London, miserably staring into shop windows and eating junk food, convinced she'd missed a golden opportunity. She had a horrible feeling her story was unfolding in a way she'd never wanted it to. That when she looked back on her life, she'd be reading from the wrong book.

The callback for a second audition came on a Tuesday morning. Her tutor met with her a few days before and was so wild with excitement that Rosa thought he might faint. He had friends at the casting agency and had heard through the grapevine they were keen to give Rosa the part. All she had to do was go back into that room on Friday and sing for them one more time – ideally without heaving like an owl trying to bring up a pellet – and the female lead in *Phantom* would be hers.

Rosa did believe in fate, but only in respect of hers being sealed. The idea that an entirely different destiny awaited her was almost too much to get her head round. On Thursday morning she bought a new dress – long, white, sweeping and romantic; perfect for Christine. On Thursday afternoon her friends found her collapsed in the kitchen of the flat they shared. She was wearing the dress, and they all thought she was dead.

Rosa woke up in hospital a few days after the audition, where a doctor looked into her yellow eyes and explained exactly how bad things were. Cystic fibrosis made the bile her liver produced sticky. It blocked the small ducts and corroded the surrounding tissue. As the damage spread, the liver became so hard blood couldn't flow through it. This had been happening inside Rosa's body for a long time, but her liver function had recently decreased so rapidly that it was now failing fast. They'd found a donor, he said, which was lucky any time but especially now. Without it, she'd only have a few days left to live.

The transplant was still loaded with peril. Rosa was weak. Even if she survived the operation, there was no guarantee it would take. It was highly possible her body would reject the new liver, and if it did the odds of them finding another workable match in what little time they had were insurmountable. To counter that, they gave Rosa immunosuppressants. These flattened her immune system to allow it to accept the new organ, but the drugs opened her up to a series of terrible infections that, because of the specifics of Rosa's condition, the doctors considered potentially more lethal than rejection of the liver itself.

After much deliberation, it was decided that Rosa's only real shot at living was for them to take her off the drugs and hope for the best. She would need to survive without medication. To rely only on a body that had always let her down. Success with these tactics was unheard of. Clive and Sandra had no idea how to tell Rosa that the role in *Phantom* had gone to somebody else, but they supposed they'd never have to. They didn't believe she would live. Instead, once more, they prepared for her to die.

It was six years later when Rosa met Ronnie in the wings of Derby Playhouse. She was just finishing up a regional tour of a musical she didn't much care about. He was appearing in the pantomime that was taking over the theatre next. She could see why they'd cast him. He was handsome and funny, blessed with magnetic charisma. Perhaps he was a little too full of himself; he wanted Aladdin and got the genie. But after a few years in a travelling company, and a series of fleeting romances in towns where it wasn't worth unpacking her suitcase, Rosa fancied a fling that might last. It was testament to Ronnie's charm that she happily watched the pantomime every evening for ten cold weeks, just to see him emerge from a wobbly cardboard lamp.

After shows they'd return to his flat, eat and have sex. He'd caress the coat hanger-shaped scar on her belly. She'd tell him all about having someone else's liver inside her, how her body had defied the predictions of all the medical professionals and accepted it entirely without drugs, allowing her to graduate, to live, to be a singer after all.

She feared, though, that her hopes of on-stage stardom were over. The chance to play Christine had been a once-in-a-lifetime opportunity. What momentum she'd built up at the Royal Academy had waned, and the handful of West End auditions she'd had since had come to nothing. Touring small productions was fine, but thanks to her illness her dreams seemed way out of reach. It was difficult to tell whether Ronnie was listening. Maybe he was lost in the graveyard of his own ambitions, like so many of the actors she met on the road.

He shrugged his shoulders when she told him cystic fibrosis had left her infertile. Three months later, when she discovered she was pregnant, those same shoulders grew heavy. Within twelve he was gone.

Beth was two years old and every bit as lively a toddler as her mother had once been when, in the autumn of 1992, Rosa walked into Ilford's Kenneth More Theatre hoping to join its small company and the pantomimes they produced. She'd desperately missed performing since becoming a mother and moving back in with her parents. This seemed like a way of rediscovering a vital part of herself.

Some of the players, Veronica especially, had been there for a long time and remembered the teenager with the bright-red lips and piercings who'd skulked in the stalls a decade or so before. She'd only heard her sing once – Rosa had been too shy to audition much back then – but she certainly recalled the impact her voice had on the tiny audience who heard it that day. It had been like watching an exotic animal wander unexpectedly into a clearing. Nobody dared move in case it bolted back to the trees.

Veronica was delighted to see Rosa return and invited her to take part in a charity concert, which is where she met Veronica's brother, Michael. That night, in her childhood bedroom as Beth slept beside her, she wrote in her diary that Michael might just be the coolest man who'd ever kissed her on the cheek.

Michael had a big silver beard that shimmered like armour in the sunlight. By day he worked a dull corporate job selling paint. At the weekend he'd pick up Rosa and Beth in the sidecar of his Harley Davidson and they'd drive around Essex with his biker gang friends. Sometimes, if Beth was lucky, he'd let her play with his collection of snakes.

By the time Rosa and Michael were married and the three of them living in his Dagenham bungalow, they'd spend entire summers camping out on land owned by the gang's leader in rural Devon. They'd drive around on quad bikes, Beth wearing short shorts, her hair glowing white. In the evening they'd light a huge bonfire and their drag queen friends would take turns to tell stories. They would beg Rosa to sing and she would always oblige them in the end.

For the first time in her life, Rosa didn't think of her death as something that lay in wait. She thought only of her daughter and how to make her next day happier than the last. As she allowed herself to conceive of a future for the first time, one appeared.

Curtain up on *Phantom* was 7.30 p.m. Rosa liked to get to the theatre by 6 to avoid the rush for hair and make-up when all the other members of the chorus arrived around 6.15. This meant collecting Beth from school at 3.25 for the brisk ten-minute walk home, then a strict forty-five minutes of homework before Michael got back from work around 4.40, depending on any traffic he hit, giving Rosa roughly seven minutes to find her shoes, make a sandwich and be on the Tube by 5. On Wednesdays, because of the matinee, the routine got so complicated that Rosa had to write it down and continually refer to it like a recipe. But she was determined to make it work. This wasn't just the realisation of a dream, it was how she'd support her daughter. It was worth the rigour and upheaval. Come showtime, all the stress and anxiety would fade away. When she finally collapsed into bed at 1 a.m. it was with music in her ears, content she was doing the very best she could.

During the summer holidays, Rosa took Beth to work with her at the theatre. Sometimes she'd watch the show from the wings with the lighting technician. At others she'd sneak behind the scenery. But Beth's favourite thing to do was to hang out in the dressing room. It was a bustling, chaotic place, where the other women in the chorus spent the time between songs loudly pulling at the knots of their lives. One was married to a man forty years older. Another was on her fourth round of IVF. A third had five children under seven and lived in a house as wild as a zoo. Beth would immerse herself in their stories, wondering how they could make them sound like such humdrum matters when to Beth they seemed like the plots of operas. She never met a single person who seemed ordinary. Everybody was so colourful and exciting. Everybody was like her mother.

In the afternoons they'd go shopping in Covent Garden. Sometimes they'd play on the arcade games at the Trocadero. They'd eat burgers and fries in hidden backstreet diners that all the West End dancers knew about but the tourists could never find. If the weather was especially good, the casts of the different musicals would meet up on Primrose Hill in the afternoons for rounders tournaments. Beth got giddy at the thought of Mr Mistoffelees throwing a fast ball, for it to be smacked by Jesus into the sky.

She dreaded the day school started again because she knew it meant she wouldn't be able to travel to London with her mother. Every time Rosa left for work without her, Beth felt cold. One afternoon she got on her bike and followed her mother to the Tube station, crying and begging her not to go. Rosa calmly explained that she had no choice. She told her this would only be going on for a little longer, and that Beth needed to be patient. But it was an act, the same act Rosa had seen her own mother perform when she'd asked her whether she was going to die before she grew up.

Because Beth was only eight, she couldn't be left alone. Michael started to call her his jailer. When she got upset he'd say it was a joke. By the time autumn came the darker evenings took on a bleak air of predictability. They ate the same dinner every night: a dire platter of instant mash, sauerkraut and limp German sausage, as though Michael was making an oblique point about the kind of slop he'd be served in an actual prison. Afterwards he'd let her watch an episode of *The Simpsons*, then send her to bed. It didn't matter that it was early or she wasn't tired. She would cry herself to sleep.

Beth was scared she'd upset her mother if she was to tell her what happened at home while she was on stage and how unhappy it was making her. She'd no idea Rosa was also feeling the blunt edges of Michael's resentment. Rosa knew his interest in her and her daughter had waned since the adventures they went on were no longer limited to the sidecar of his motorcycle. On the colder, darker days, if he mustered the energy to speak to her at all, it was only to belittle her, a kind of revenge he liked to enact for the crime of ruining his life. She had seen this switch in men before – she'd seen it in Ronnie when she got pregnant – as though their blood was poisoned when something came along in her life that they had no power to control.

One day, Rosa sat Beth down and told her that she was desperately sad in her marriage. It wasn't unusual for her to burden her daughter with adult matters. Beth already understood herself to be her mother's confidante, even if she was too young to measure the depth of her feelings. Rosa had raised her for this; to be the friend she'd never had, the one fixed point in a curtailed life. She promised her that, whatever happened next, they would be together. They didn't need anyone else. From now on, it would be just the two of them. Beth straddled a suitcase so that Rosa could seal its catch. They each gripped the handle and dragged it out through the door.

There were other houses. A bungalow here. A maisonette there. There were walls that changed so frequently Beth forgot what it was to come home. For a while, they shared a sofa bed in a Dagenham studio flat. Beth adored the Sundays they'd spend under the duvet, watching films and eating biscuits. But as Monday approached she would grow sullen. By the evening, Rosa found that no amount of home-made cookies could put a smile on Beth's face.

Other men came along. Beth was twelve when Rosa and Bruce bought a house in Whitstable. It had stairs and a garden and separate bedrooms, things so novel to Beth that for the first few months of living there it felt as though they'd moved into a museum of normal family life. Sometimes, when she ate a bowl of cornflakes, she couldn't shake the feeling she'd be told off for touching the exhibit. Everything seemed too perfect, and Beth sometimes wondered if Bruce felt the same way. Here was another actor, a kindly man, adrift around the periphery of amateur touring productions, suddenly finding himself with a beautiful home in a charming seaside town, loved by a woman and daughter who'd been lost until he came into their lives. He was warm and attentive. Beth didn't know what it was like to have a father, but she imagined it was something like this – something sturdy beneath you, to always feel sure of foot. She couldn't wait to tell him she'd aced her exams, but when she ran home from school that day he and his things were gone.

Rosa would leave Beth's dinner in the slow cooker, and while Rosa was at the theatre Beth looked after herself: getting back from school, eating, washing up, doing her homework, watching TV and falling asleep on the sofa. When Rosa came home at 1 a.m. she'd always find Beth there, dappled by the manic light of cartoons. Sitting down. Stroking Beth's hair. Rosa's breath short and shorter still. The familiar rattle of infection in her lungs and no choice but to stop.

Beth walked into the new flat her mother had chosen for them, saw the small, dark rooms, heard the neighbours arguing through the walls and immediately decided it wasn't just a mistake, it was a catastrophe. For the first time in her life she had a tight group of friends at school in Whitstable, and in 2011 every single one of them rightly thought Margate was a fucking dump. Nothing about the mould in the corners, the musty-smelling bedrooms or the burger-featured youths patrolling the shitty streets outside would prove them wrong. People talked about how the area would be transformed once the Turner Contemporary opened, but it didn't seem like that to Beth. The way she saw it, she'd made it to the cusp of womanhood and here she was, committing social suicide. She was sixteen and wanted an exciting career in fashion and a sexy, funny boyfriend. Now she'd have more chance of both if she washed her hair in dung.

Even though she didn't quite believe it, Rosa assured Beth everything would work out fine. In many ways, all of these concerns were irrelevant. Margate might have been a town on its knees, but it was the only place where they could afford a home. That was why artists and single-parent families were beginning to arrive in droves. It had been a struggle to find regular work since quitting *Phantom*. Her degree didn't qualify her to teach in schools, and private vocal coaching only just kept the lights on. She loved the work – nothing gave her greater pleasure than singing every day – but she spent as many hours cajoling clients to pay her on time as she did guiding them through the scales. A series of loans had kept them afloat until the bank threatened to repossess the house. Now she'd no choice but to sell it, and by the time she'd cleared her debts there was barely anything left. Margate was the only place in Britain, in the world, they could go.

Rosa tried to hide the worst of her money worries from Beth like she tried to hide the truth of her love life. Recently she'd been experimenting with online dating. A few flings came out of it, with younger men mostly, so to Beth her mother's romantic adventures looked remarkably successful. She was always going on dates and coming home with flowers. But for Rosa the early days of each new relationship were tinged with sadness. She could hide but not deny the fact that she was getting sicker. It would be cruel to take a lover down this road with her. It was hard enough with a daughter. The moment she felt things were getting serious she would call it off for some made-up reason, unable to declare what it really was – an act of mercy they'd never be able to appreciate.

Nor did she tell Beth the full truth about her visits to Brompton Hospital. They weren't lies exactly; it would have been impossible to disguise the fact that she was having treatment more frequently, and Beth couldn't help but notice the new drugs which kept appearing in the medicine cabinet or the way Rosa grew short of breath walking to the bus stop. But Rosa shrugged off the calls from the doctor, and talked about the regular endoscopies she endured as though she was off to get her hair done again.

When she wasn't sick, Rosa and Beth spent all of their time together. They enjoyed watching TV, cooking and making clothes. For their birthdays they'd compete to see who could make the other the most ridiculous card. They'd write each other poems and love letters. Neither of them could quite remember how or why the tradition began, but they'd randomly send one another photographs of the actress Cameron Diaz, imagining the smile they'd be greeted with when the envelopes were opened up.

On the rare occasions when she was alone, Rosa looked for new ways to pay the bills. Margate proved to be an ideal place for her eccentric kind of industriousness. There might have been little in the way of conventional employment on offer, but she'd never been a conventional woman. It was edifying to find herself in the middle of a growing community of artists, musicians and bohemians using their talents to get by. Rosa and Beth spent a summer running family fun days for an events company, painting children's faces outside McDonald's and splitting the cash. Beth perfected tiger stripes. Rosa learnt to make an entire bicycle out of balloons. In the evenings she joined a 1980s cover band and played gigs all over Thanet. Sometimes she'd cough up blood before she went on stage to sing, her pockets full of tissues stained red.

Rosa was used to concerned expressions on the faces of doctors. She'd seen enough of them over the past fifty-three years. This one, though, was different. He said her liver seemed a bit stiff, that the cirrhosis might have returned, but if it had these were very early days and they could monitor the situation closely. Rosa tried to hide it from Beth. She pretended the tests they'd ordered for her kidneys were routine, because she didn't want to spoil her daughter's happiness.

Beth had been happier than Rosa had ever known her since Rosa introduced her to Jon, a talented young musician she met at a gig the year before. Rosa couldn't bear to sully those heady early days of their relationship by making Beth worry about her health, especially when there was a decent chance it would pass like it always did in the end and the tests would come back clear.

For most of Beth's life the decline in Rosa's health had been so gradual as to be imperceptible, so painful as to be best ignored, something Beth would watch but never see. But since they moved to Margate her illness had been unrelenting. Beth had lost count of the number of times she'd come home to find her mother collapsed, sweating and shaking on the floor, in the grip of a diabetic hypo so savage she could barely remember her name. Beth's answer was to try and make Rosa as happy as she possibly could. She knew nothing would do that more than seeing her daughter in the kind of relationship that had always eluded her. One lasting and true. To know that she was loved.

Even by the standards of a Spanish summer it was a beautiful day when Beth proposed to Jon in a Barcelona park. She'd had the ring specially made. He'd not suspected a thing. They sent Rosa a photograph of the two of them together with the caption 'getting married', knowing she was on her way to a medical appointment and that the news would make her smile at exactly the moment she needed it most. That evening they ate tapas and celebrated in a bar on the lip of the Gothic Quarter, which was where they were, full of love, empanadas and champagne, when Beth got a call from her aunty Gloria saying that Rosa was in hospital, and this time it was bad.

Two of the consultants at the Intensive Care Unit remembered Rosa from their days as medical students. To them she was the woman who'd had a liver transplant without the use of immunosuppressant drugs and not just survived, but thrived. Not one of the men who'd been involved in her treatment, many of whom would go on to become specialists in the field, had ever dared predict this. Rosa was such a memorable anomaly that they still referred to her when training new staff. Her story had become a neat way of reminding junior doctors how much of what they were about to learn could be humbled by the human will to live.

Rosa remained in hospital for another three months. Beth stayed at home alone, anxiously fielding phone calls from nurses over Christmas. She knew that beyond regular visits there was nothing she could do to help, but the sense of powerlessness was overwhelming, and it only grew with each setback, each mishandled development.

One night, Rosa's oesophageal varices started to bleed. There were no doctors on duty and the bleeds were not immediately recognised. Instead of being sedated so that they could be cauterised and bound, she was returned to ICU and intubated, anaesthetised so that a breathing tube could be forced down through the already shredded walls of her throat. It felt to Beth like Rosa had been chosen as a guinea pig to demonstrate how overworked and under-resourced the NHS was. When the nurses forgot to tape Rosa's eyelids down while she was unconscious, the harsh strip lighting on the ceiling scorched her retinas. Beth wept. But, like the specialists decades before, she'd grossly underestimated her mother's will to go on.

Rosa knew she had a catalogue of chronic problems. Her liver was failing. She would need to have her stomach drained frequently, and the more that happened, the worse it would be. Her kidneys were also giving up, so she would require regular dialysis for the rest of her life. Cut it whichever way, she was extremely sick. But it was the good news she rushed to tell Beth: they were going to put her on the transplant list. The sense of pride she felt was tremendous. This was what she had been fighting so hard for over the last three months, and she'd achieved it.

Beth was delighted. She assumed, from what Rosa told her, that the monitoring of the liver would from now on be so thorough that the moment it failed they'd whip it out and replace it with one that worked, like they had before, before she was born. She was undoubtedly ill and the future would be tough, but they still had options.

She didn't know what Rosa knew and was hiding. There was no way they were going to give her another liver. It would be a waste of a perfectly good organ. Her place on the transplant list was a lie she'd wanted to hear for her daughter, so that Beth would have something to cling to, a log in a river that had swept them away

Rosa was too ill to work, and Beth was attempting to set up a business selling second-hand vintage clothes that – if it paid out – wouldn't do so for months. In between driving Rosa to regular hospital appointments and filling in endless application forms for Personal Independence Payment, she'd no chance of making money. Rosa had always been against the idea of taking handouts from the state, but Beth reminded her of their stark reality: multiple organ failure and toast for lunch again. If she was going to care for her mother like her mother once cared for her, then she was going to need cash. Especially in the absence of friends.

As they watched Prime Minister Boris Johnson announce that Britain was going into lockdown, it was as though the situation had been designed specifically for their torment. Rosa only had the shell of an immune system. Travelling to and from hospital on patient transport three times a week gave what was once a simple journey the potential to be her last. But at least she could leave the flat. Beth couldn't go anywhere in case she brought the virus back. There would be no visits from their family, or from Jon, who lived with his own elderly parents. So it was just the two of them, together, just like it had always been.

They spent their days making food Rosa fancied but could never eat. After dinner they'd squabble over what to watch on TV. Rosa always won. Her illness gave her special licence to demand another episode of *Law & Order*, and Beth had the grace to concede. Anyway, it wouldn't be on for long before Rosa fell asleep once more, her head on Beth's lap, Beth stroking the velvety fuzz of her mother's shaven scalp in flickering bluish light.

She would hope tomorrow might be a day when they'd laugh again, not give in to the tension that made them say nasty, regrettable things. One morning Rosa told the patient transport driver that she hated everything Beth cooked. Beth overheard and called her mother an ungrateful fucking bitch. Rosa shot back that Beth was a silly little cow. They both slammed their bedroom doors and didn't speak for the rest of the week. Come Saturday it was like it had never happened.

*

There's a photograph. It's May. Rosa's fifty-fourth birthday. Beth, with her mouth twisted towards Rosa's face as if to kiss her, Rosa's red lipstick hot against the yellow of her skin. Behind them the kitchen is small and falling apart. There is a cake they made but didn't eat and balloons taped to the wall. There is deep love in dimming eyes.

She would tell someone all about her mother's life one day. How Rosa cared for Beth so Beth cared for Rosa. There was comfort in understanding life as a loop. That the end is a hand held out to the beginning. That the beginning holds in it the end.

Thirteen

Towards the end of January I finally gave in to my sons' incessant demands to buy them a set of sinkers, tubes of colourful weighted plastic that you throw into a pool in order to retrieve them from the bottom. A boy they'd befriended on holiday had let them play with his, and they'd done so all day without getting bored, which seemed miraculous at the time. Sinkers had since become such a preoccupation in our household that it was as though he'd introduced them to cigarettes. Their desire to have their own had morphed into a kind of mania, leaving me with no choice. That afternoon we sat together on the sofa with my laptop open, scrolling through the available options on eBay. While they argued over which ones to get – sinkers designed like torpedoes or sinkers designed like sharks – my eyes drifted across the other open browser windows. Twelve were devoted to the search for Caroline Lane.

My efforts to find out more about Caroline had stalled. While Beth's experience with management companies had given me a welcome new perspective on Caroline's character, and being in the physical space of her flat had helped me imagine her more vividly, nobody had turned up to collect the money from the sale of the property. Meanwhile, all my other leads were meeting dead ends. I'd run out of ideas, and was beginning to fear the worst – that her story would fade into obscurity. Though it was mostly fruitless, endlessly scouring the internet for traces of Caroline became the only way I had of fending off a gnawing sense of disquiet. While it was a comfort to me, it was aggravating my family. Even Lou's patience was being tested by the whole endeavour, especially when I found myself absent-mindedly scrolling at the dinner table. Like a dog fixated on a shadow, I couldn't stop.

We settled on sinkers designed to look like the Beatles' yellow submarine. This pleased my youngest son, who was five years old and had recently developed an obsession with the assassination of John Lennon that might have matched mine with Caroline had he been able to get online. They returned to the TV show they'd been watching as I placed a bid. It was then, with my cursor blinking in the search bar, that I realised something. It jolted me upright in my seat.

While I'd tried every search engine and social media platform I could think of in my hunt for Caroline, most of them many times, I had never entered her name into eBay. I always experienced a rush of excitement when a new avenue to explore presented itself, no matter how unlikely the chances of success. It felt like being marooned on a desert island and seeing a passing ship.

My joy was short-lived. There were no results. Or at least no results that could conceivably be anything to do with the Caroline Lane I was looking for. The same was true when I entered her father's name, Bert. So when I entered the name of Caroline's mother, Norma Lane, it was having slumped back against the cushion, feeling a little foolish for having got my hopes up again. My attention was already turning back to the sinkers and my insulting opening bid.

I was only half paying attention, but as I skimmed through the results something caught my eye: a black and white photograph of a woman. She had a brilliant smile, bright eyes and a coat with a lavish fur collar. It would be an understatement to say she was chic; she looked like a mid-twentieth-century Hollywood starlet, sharing more than a passing resemblance to the actress Natalie Wood. The photograph was part of a cutting of a newspaper article published in 1975 which was being sold for £5 by a man named Jerry Carmichael. Beneath it was a headline I read three or four times, with a growing sense of astonishment and elation. It said, simply: NORMA MAKES WAVES.

There was a trace of Caroline Lane online. Her sole digital footprint had come about in the most analogue of ways, the past peeking gently through the now.

Jerry Carmichael lived on a rugged stretch of the Northumberland coast. After his wife Patricia retired she became interested in tracing her family tree. This wasn't so simple as it might have seemed at first. Much of her family history was rooted in rural Australia, where historic public records could be difficult to come by. However, she'd recently found an enterprising businessman there who, if she gave him dates, names and locations, would, after a wait of a month or two, send her a package of photocopies of any newspaper articles he could find related to her family for a payment of £90.

Jerry thought it quite a lot of money for a service like this. But it also gave him an idea. Like Patricia, he had been looking for interesting ways to spend his retirement. And, because of his previous job at a printers, he had access to an enormous trove of old newspapers that were currently rotting away in storage. Armed with time and resources, Jerry started cutting out random articles and listing them on eBay. It was a strange pastime, and one that, unbeknown to him, would soon become an obsession in itself.

His cuttings weren't photocopies, they were originals, so he priced them accordingly, at £5 or £6 a piece. They didn't need to feature celebrities or famous events for him to cut them out and put them up for sale. They didn't need to be bizarre, or newsworthy, or even especially interesting. They were just things that caught his eye. To Jerry, that was the beauty of the whole endeavour. It didn't matter what it was, or how boring or unimportant it seemed. He knew that everyone had a unique life experience. What meant nothing to him meant something to someone. We all have a story to tell.

He'd list them with a brief summary of their contents. For instance: '1912 Ireland's Cheerfullest Newsboy, Tony O'Flaherty Of Tralee'. Or '1953 Thousands Of Dead Fish Washed Up At Provincetown, Massachusetts Refuse To Burn'. Or '1909 Abnormal Night-time Activities Of James McCaltry, 154 Bristol Road'. Most never found a buyer. But some did. He'd sold articles to all sorts of interesting people: a Hollywood screenwriter deep in research for a script. Buckingham Palace staff hoping to fill holes in their archives. Businesses. Pubs. Collectors. Museums all over the world. And thousands of appreciative individuals, all looking for something nobody else was, something lost in the past. Some sold years after they were listed. Some sold within hours. There was never any way of knowing what would get bought and what wouldn't. But if he just left an article up for sale, there was always a chance that someone, somewhere, would stumble upon it in their search for a missing piece.

When Jerry listed an article he titled '1975 Glamorous Mrs Norma Lane Brings Pizazz To Fashion Parade', he was right about one thing. Norma was definitely glamorous. The article read like this:

NORMA MAKES WAVES

We are in the grip of such a cold spell at the moment that only the most fashion conscious female might get in a twist about spring fashions. But glamorous MRS. NORMA LANE (pictured above) is already planning her spring outfit. The 'Lady of Fashion' competition is to take place in March, and Norma has won her way through to the finals.

32-year-old Norma knows as well as any 'lady of fashion' that winning isn't cheap. Finding the pizazz to win is proving quite the expense.

'Every heat requires a new outfit. The first heat was months ago and that required a summer outfit. I needed a winter outfit for the semi-finals last week. So of course I'll be thinking about spring for the finals', said Norma, a mother of three children, Caroline, Meredith and Simon, the eldest of whom is 12.

Offering my assistance, I suggested she consider her show-stopping emerald green number with a shimmering floral midi-skirt that the judges greatly admired.

'Goodness, no. Never for spring. I think a pastel coloured affair might suit, don't you? . . .' Her voice trailed off dreamily.

Who can blame her? Perhaps half the fun is buying new clothes.

Two days later, the article arrived through my door in a neat plastic folder. The paper had yellowed slightly, but up close Norma's beauty beamed from the page. I'd never seen a photograph of Caroline beyond the brief, pixelated glimpse of one I'd managed to freeze-frame in the video of Dee and the others entering her flat. But Leonard, Mrs Bennett (and Bert and Janet, the current directors of the Saltwater Mansions management company who'd seen the photograph in her bedroom that day) had, in not dissimilar terms, described her to me as having high cheekbones and round, dark eyes with a mischievous glint. The image of her that had since formed in my imagination was now vivid enough that Norma's face in the article felt strangely familiar, like someone I'd met before but couldn't quite remember when or where.

The 'Lady of Fashion' competition was a beauty contest run by a holiday camp in Prestatyn. Every year they published a brochure to entice the next season's holidaymakers. For this purpose they always devoted a page to recapping the previous season's highlights. A woman named Penny, who holidayed there regularly during this time and looked back on it with great fondness, had in adulthood chosen to sell her collection of these brochures on eBay, just as Jerry had the random newspaper articles. Leafing through the 1976 edition meant I could say for sure that, having sailed through to the final in 1975, Norma was unlucky not to win the top prize: a silver trophy, £200 cash and a trip for two to the home of haute couture, Paris, where, according to the article, she might have fitted right in.

In the 1970s, newspapers tended to advertise their sexist attitudes even more freely than they do today. It was hard, though not impossible, to imagine a report on a beauty contest now, let alone one that made such a big deal of the fact that a thirty-two-year-old finalist had three children, with the oldest being twelve, or that her voice trailed off dreamily at the end of a sentence about pastel-coloured spring suits. Though outmoded, these transgressions were undeniably useful for my purposes. That there was a Norma Lane with a daughter named Caroline who might have been exactly the same age as the Caroline that left Saltwater Mansions in 2009 seemed too big a coincidence to ignore.

When I finally fell asleep that night, it was with the article on my bedside table, enthralled by what now seemed not just possible but true. If the glamorous woman in the photograph was Caroline's mother, and she had three children in 1975, it meant that Caroline had two siblings. And if that was the case, it meant that maybe there was someone out there who knew Caroline more intimately than anyone who'd lived at Saltwater Mansions ever did. Someone I might now be able to find.

The next morning I woke prepared for what I presumed would be a full day of sifting through public records and search results. I was wrong. Finding Meredith and Simon would not take a full day or anything like that long. Within an hour I had their birth and marriage records printed out and arranged around my desk. I knew when and where they were born (in different parts of the country to Caroline; they'd moved around as children), when and where they were married (Simon had been married twice), as well as specific details about his divorce. By lunchtime, I'd so much information about them I'd run out of desk space and begun to tack it to the walls. Standing back to survey my findings, I could confidently assume a decent understanding of the rough shape of their lives. When I did there was one discovery that struck me as especially poignant. Simon was once the director of a limited company to which he'd given his father's name. Caroline's family had, at some point in the past, either with or without her, been close.

If anything, piecing Meredith and Simon's stories together was too easy. Doing it left me cold. Caroline's story was alluring precisely because it was a mystery. The ins and outs of her life were as difficult to grasp as the darkness where they seemed to determined to stay. In that respect, she represented a throwback to a bygone age, one left behind since the internet granted us access to what was once obscured. This was partly why I'd fallen down the rabbit hole in the first place.

By contrast, searching for glimpses of Meredith's and Simon's stories was a clinical and calculated process, so much so that engaging in it felt more like an act of anti-curiosity. It was as though they were from a different world to their sister, and that what came next would mean tearing a hole through the thin barrier that, possibly for good reason, separated the two.

It now seemed inevitable that I would need to break the news of Caroline's disappearance – and with it the very real probability she was dead – to one of her siblings. Given that neither Meredith nor Simon had appeared at Saltwater Mansions after Caroline vanished, it seemed likely there had been an estrangement of some kind. A rupture that meant they didn't know about their sister's fate, or didn't care. There were plenty of reasons why a family might drift apart over a period of time. I'd seen enough of my friends' families break up to make me sometimes think of their individual members as being like tectonic plates, shifting fragments of a volatile mass.

As I considered what these ruptures might have been, and how upsetting it could be to be forced to revisit them, the dread I felt at the thought of making contact with Meredith and Simon Lane began to swell again. I couldn't comprehend a scenario where what I did next wouldn't be devastating in some way. If somebody informed me that my sister was missing, presumed dead, after I'd had no contact with her for many years, I would be heartbroken no matter what had gone on between us in the past. It felt as though I was about to deliver a bomb.

If I was assuaged by anything it was that, at first glance, contacting Meredith or Simon seemed every bit as impossible as contacting their sister. I couldn't find any current addresses or active social media accounts. In fact, if it wasn't for the fact that I remembered Meredith from my childhood, it might all have stopped there. Maybe I would have felt relieved.

It's here that I hit something of a snag. Meredith is famous. Or at least, she used to be, insomuch as these things can be measured. What's beyond doubt is that she was a pop star. There was a period of about a year in the mid- to late 1980s when I remember her music blasting out from my sister's bedroom on an almost daily basis, sandwiched between plays of 'Sometimes' by Erasure and the *Dirty Dancing* soundtrack. On some deep, Pavlovian level, I associate the sound of Meredith's singing with my sister getting ready to go out, and me desperately wishing I was old enough to do the same.

The snag is this. While I have changed certain names and identifying details, everything you've read so far has been true. And everything you're yet to read will to all intents and purposes be true too. But unless I disguise Meredith's identity, you might well know who she is. Especially if you are of a certain age. If you don't know who she is, it would definitely be possible to go online and find out. And you might, because the nature of how we engage with stories like this one has changed in profound and unsteadying ways. Ready access to a whole world of information has activated the traditionally passive audience. Trying to find out supplementary information about anyone or anything is now part and parcel of how we consume stories. The problem is that the internet's promise of truth has created a world anything but truthful.

If someone was so minded, they might want to find out more about Meredith than I am willing to share here in the hope of discovering something about Caroline that I have failed to find. But Meredith, much like her sister, is a private person. While it's true that the details of her life were well chronicled during the period of her fame, that period was brief. It probably only lasted for two or three years. Since then, she has guarded her privacy so fiercely that there are more websites devoted to conjecture about what became of her than there are sources of accurate information. She doesn't share selfies or holiday snaps or posts about going wild swimming. By modern standards, Meredith, like Caroline, is something of an enigma.

Anybody curious enough to search for more detail about Caroline by delving into the life of Meredith will probably find that their curiosity goes unsatisfied. Indeed, there are so few details to be found that it might seem like things don't make sense, that something is missing, or certain areas of intrigue don't add up as expected. They might interpret what they don't find as proof of something that isn't there and jump to false conclusions, writing their own version of this story and creating a parallel reality. A life that didn't exist. Another iteration of Caroline Lane.

So I am going to blur the lines around what comes next to prevent this from happening. Though the following is fundamentally true, I am going to use some creative licence with regards to Meredith that I might not otherwise have employed. I'm aware that this is an act of some hypocrisy on my part. After all, the thing I am seeking to stop is only that which I have already done.

*

Meredith's fame might have been short-lived, but while it lasted she received an intense level of attention. She was a regular fixture in the tabloids and there was a moment, as her popularity was at its apex, when she must have felt like she didn't have much of a private life at all. Her story had become public property.

She gave many interviews during this time. In the ones I was able to find, Meredith frequently mentioned her family, and always in glowing terms. While she never used Caroline's name, there were occasional, fond references to her sister. In one she said they were 'best friends', which might be the kind of thing pop stars say to interviewers from teen magazines on their thirteenth such encounter of the day, but it was clear that, particularly as young women in the 1980s, Meredith and Caroline got on well and liked to spend time together, when and where they could.

Meredith wasn't in show business any more. One message board devoted to chronicling the lives of former pop stars carried a short post that confidently claimed she now lived in the countryside and was married to an architect. However, she had retained an agent, and would occasionally appear at signing events, selling autographed photos to nostalgic punters who, like me, remembered her from their youth.

I felt a little embarrassed highlighting the fact that I'd had some books published before as a reason to consider me legitimate, but I had precious little else working in my favour when it came to persuading former pop stars to talk to me. So I emailed the agent some links to the kinder reviews of my previous book and asked if I might contact Meredith in the name of research for a forthcoming project I was working on. They responded quickly. It wouldn't be a problem at all.

Having Meredith's email address only made the anxieties I had about writing to her even worse. For a period of about a week, I tried to convince myself that my obsession with trying to tell Caroline's story had been an enormous folly, as though I might be able to undermine it and make it go away. It didn't work. The more I denied it, the more it grew.

In the end I decided that, had Caroline been my sister, I would want to know that she had disappeared no matter the state of our relationship. Still, I continually wrote and rewrote the email over the next two weeks, desperate to find an elusive string of words that might soften the blow of their meaning, or at least negate the fear I had about all of these things. I wanted it to be compassionate and kind, to be in no way sensational or gratuitous, to not put Meredith in mind of the kind of journalists she might understandably have tired of back when her life was tabloid fodder. Ultimately, though, I had to accept that there's no adequate way to visit loss on somebody. It was best to keep it brief.

> *Dear Meredith,*
> *I am a writer who for the last six months has been looking into the forced sale of a flat in Margate. The flat had been vacant for 13 years after the owner vanished without trace, leaving behind all of her possessions which have now been sold, donated or destroyed. It is with regret I write to inform you that it is my belief she was your sister, Caroline Lane.*
> *Yours,*
> *David*

One night, when it was late and I was alone, I pressed send. It was hard to fall asleep afterwards, and in the hours I lay awake I was unable to shake myself free of the guilt that I had just broken the hearts of a stranger and her family. But

I still wanted to know who Caroline had been. And now that I had made contact with someone who knew her, I took solace in the fact that I might find out. If I hoped for anything, it was this: that the story of the woman who disappeared would not disappear too.

In the morning I made a pot of coffee, and while I waited for it to brew I checked my phone. Meredith had replied.

Dear David,
Thank you for your email.
  Its contents have come as a tremendous shock to me. It is difficult to know how to respond. I want to give this some thought.
  I just need to speak to Caroline first.
  Yours,
  Meredith

My heart sped up and I could feel my face turning hot, as if all of the blood in my body was collecting in my cheeks. I ran through to the lounge, where Lou was engaged in the never-ending negotiation with our children over turning the TV down, and thrust the phone in front of her face. She read Meredith's email twice and asked if I was joking. I assured her I wasn't. Caroline was alive. I appeared to have found a woman who'd vanished. A woman even private detectives couldn't track down. The woman who, over these last six months, had become a mysterious, dominant figure in my life.

For the first few hours of that chilly Saturday morning, the news that Caroline wasn't dead was too huge to fully compute. Besides shock, my first reaction was elation. I hadn't conceived of an outcome like this, certainly not one that would mean my concerns about her story being forgotten were unfounded. For that, and the fact that she was in touch with people who (I hoped) loved her, I felt a tremendous sense of relief.

I was also confused. I'd imagined dozens of versions of Caroline Lane's story, but there wasn't one which began with her disappearing without trace and ended in her now being with or at least around her family, living what might have been a completely 'ordinary' life. I had been so preoccupied with ensuring her story was not forgotten, I'd never allowed myself to believe she hadn't been forgotten at all. I was reminded of the books my children had enjoyed when they were younger, where separate parts of the illustrations could be flipped independently of each other so the reader could create different animals (a tiger's head on the body of a duck, a chimp's legs beneath the top half of a llama). The two parts together didn't make sense.

Regardless, it was an exhilarating revelation. The rest of the weekend was lost to fantasies of sitting down with Caroline and learning about her in her own words. In these daydreams we would finally meet in a fancy restaurant, where she would gently answer the questions I came back to over and over again in my mind. Why had she left? Why did she never return? Why had she continued to pay her mortgage? Why didn't she sell the flat? And through them I might come to an answer to the biggest question, the one that underpinned it all: who are you?

Even so, these suddenly seemed like minor mysteries compared to the one I was only now beginning to comprehend. All of the time I'd been searching for Caroline, it had never occurred to me that she hadn't disappeared from Saltwater Mansions at all. The 'tremendous shock' Meredith expressed in her email was not the result of me telling her Caroline was missing or might be dead, because to Meredith

Caroline was neither. She was very much alive. She was down the road, or on the other end of a phone. The actual source of her shock seemed to be me informing her that Caroline's flat had been forcibly sold, and that everything inside it had since been donated, sold or destroyed. This suggested not only that Meredith did not know about the forced sale, but that she hadn't been aware of the flat's existence in the first place. She'd no idea Caroline lived in Saltwater Mansions, or maybe even in Margate at all. This, not her sister's vanishing, was the mystery for Meredith. This was the thing that couldn't be explained.

Could it be the case that the four years during which Caroline lived in flat nine, Saltwater Mansions was the time she spent disappeared from somewhere else? Her relatives didn't seem to know where she'd gone when she moved there in 2005. If she'd walked out of their lives, they could not reasonably have expected to find her in a flat in a run-down seaside town like Margate in the mid-2000s. A forgotten, crumbling, unloved British coastal resort lost in the hinterland between desolation and transformation was somewhere nobody would look for her. It wasn't just the perfect place to vanish from. It was the perfect place to vanish to.

Could it be that in this version of her story – on the day shortly after the 2009 AGM when Caroline walked out of the front door of Saltwater Mansions for a final time, leaving clothes on the clothes horse and food in the fridge and the bedsheets still holding her shape, while Mr Peake was writing his resignation letter citing her unreasonable behaviour and Mr Curtis was licking the envelope on the first of many pleas for her to pay her share of the fire escape renovation – Caroline was being welcomed back into a loving family who for four years had missed her in ways that caused them unimaginable anguish? While I'd been searching in the shadows, had she been lying in the sun?

Caroline sits in her favourite armchair, calmed by the view of a garden that shimmers as the light skulks in segments across the lawn. These days, it's the simple things that give her most joy: the head bob of wild flowers, dogfighting butterflies, swifts returning on tired, pretty wings. Even the sight of her neighbour's cat clawing at the rose bed doesn't irk her in the way it might once have done, back then. She still shoos it away of course – this isn't a pet shop – but not without a smile that yields to its charms. She wraps a fine cashmere blanket tight around her legs and for a while she paints the sunset. Nothing soothes her like an orangey dusk, the sound of the birds and the gentle scratch of canvas under brush.

Later she'll retire to the sofa and read. She's still not the type to persevere with a novel if it hasn't grabbed her within fifty pages. Life's too precious to spend with bad literature. Every third Thursday, at her book club, she'll loudly wonder what it was everyone else enjoyed about the book so much. Whether she's the only person there with any sense. They all laugh about it afterwards. Typical Caroline, they say. Forthright and funny and frightening the newcomers. They wouldn't want and can't imagine her any other way. Deep down she likes them, even if it doesn't always come across that way.

Caroline folds the corner of the page and shuffles through into the kitchen to make a chicken soup with the leeks she grew herself. Back when she was young and naive, on the rare occasions when she had cause to imagine approaching old age, this little flat was not the home where she envisaged ending up. That would have been a large West London apartment with a wide, art-filled hallway, a black piano. Or a sprawling pile in the Sussex Downs. A converted oast house maybe, the kind you'd find on postcards, with outbuildings, stables and endless lush green hills. It's funny, how back then she saw life as a long straight line. How she was blind to the chicanery ahead. That's what living is, she supposes: not noticing the bends until you're facing in another direction. Who you are is how you deal with the next of your new views.

She peels garlic. Slower than she'd like. The joints of her fingers ache. But she licks the tip of one to turn the pages of *The Times* she has splayed out on the table. She likes to read while she cooks, to murmur to herself about the things she sees in the news. Sometimes it seems as though the world is collapsing in on itself. When did it become OK for politicians to squabble like schoolboys? Why must people in restaurants always be on their phones? What in God's name are young women doing with their eyebrows? She's not especially given to nostalgia, but she's quite sure things would improve tenfold if taking a photograph of your own face wasn't so much of a thing.

Her sister, her lovely sister, would say she's softened with age, and maybe she has. She's mellower and more patient than she used to be. Here, where she lives, where she moved to be closer to her family (she'll never forget how readily they opened their arms and welcomed her home when she needed them most), it's so quiet she sometimes sings to herself in the morning when she wakes just to check she's not gone deaf. But she still snaps at the delivery men when they manhandle her packages. And she's not afraid to fire off a letter of complaint where it's due. She doesn't know it, but they've a nickname for her at the local council.

Bubbles pulse through the soup on the hob. She wishes she had an AGA; there's enough for four but it'll keep.

Radio 4 is usually on in the background, filling the flat with conversation that makes her forget she's alone. She doesn't get many visitors these days, but she has enough friends she keeps at a distance, where she likes them to be. Some of the women at the WI probably think her a bit offish for such crimes as not wanting to get involved in the Christmas garland-making workshop. But she's really quite fun beneath the veneer. They all say they love the lemon cake she makes and the naughty sound of her laugh. Age hasn't slowed her wit any more than it's blunted her tongue.

The slow dance of the steam brings her gaze to the middle distance, her mind to memories that draw her from the room. She's never been the type to look back, and she doesn't plan on starting now, in the autumn of her years. There are things she'd rather forget. (And she has, in a way. Like the flat. Put it all to the back of her mind so that she might go on.) But, if she had to?

It didn't all go her way, of course. If it had, she'd never have ended up in Margate. It all feels like a blip now, an unwanted interruption, but the things that happened to her happened and the choices she made were the choices she made and the people she met were the people she met. Life comes and it comes and all you can do is hope it doesn't erode you like waves do the cliffs she used to see from her window every morning. Would she do things differently if she had the chance again? Of course. But a life is written in indelible ink.

When she thinks of Saltwater Mansions now, it's as a spent chrysalis from which she once emerged. Her story is not why she went there in the first place. Nor is it who she was when she was there, or why, in the end, she left it behind. Her story is one of survival. The stories of all lives are. At least she'll never have to tell it; her family know better than to ever ask her that.

She tears apart a slice of crusty bread and mops up what remains of the soup. The colours and patterns on the bottom of the bowl are better than anything she's captured on her easel today. The phone rings. Meredith already called twice before this afternoon, she's probably wondering where Caroline has disappeared to, so she mumbles to herself as she moves through into the lounge, where she likes to leave her mobile on the coffee table, as far away as possible. Out of sight, out of mind. This time, though, she'd better answer it. To find out what her beloved sister deems so urgent as this.

I waited weeks for Meredith to respond again, as she had said she would once she had given it some thought. My biggest hope was that Caroline was doing the same, that my email to her sister might pique her curiosity as she had mine, and she might write to me too. This did not happen. I spent a month continually checking my inbox. Nothing came.

Eventually, when I was unable to resist any longer, I sat at my desk and wrote a long letter to Caroline that I requested Meredith pass on. It seemed important to explain how I came to find her, in the hope that it dispelled any worries she might have about my intentions. I said it would have been reasonable for Caroline to assume my motives were sinister, or at least untoward. But I wasn't fishing for gossip about her famous sister. Nor was I angling for a share of the £100,000 I believed was sitting in a government pot somewhere after the forced sale of her property, like an elaborate scam artist. None of these things were my concern.

I wanted to tell her that, while she might not have regarded leaving Saltwater Mansions as a disappearance, there were those who did. For Dee, Leonard, Beth, Mrs Bennett, Ruby, Bert, Janet and the other residents, Caroline had always been in their thoughts. Whether she knew it or not, she had not been forgotten. And the truth, I wrote, was that ever since I first heard about her she'd been in my thoughts too. I wanted her to know that, in some small way, she'd been missed. This might sound odd to someone who didn't even know they'd vanished, but the reason, I said, why I'd spent the last six months looking for her was because I couldn't bear the thought that her story had gone with her. Now that it was clear this wasn't the case, I wondered if, finally, she might tell it to me.

Meredith thanked me for my letter. She said she had passed it on to Caroline and she'd no doubt my intentions were good. They were grateful to me for bringing the matter of the forced sale of her flat to their attention. But Caroline, she said, did not want to talk to me, and would not be persuaded otherwise. Out of loyalty to her sister, which overrode all else, Meredith said she could no longer communicate with me either. Her email ended with words that, afterwards, I knew would always haunt me, to a greater or lesser degree.

'I just want you to know that Caroline is a nice person.'

Fourteen

It was a bright, clear February morning when I went to Saltwater Mansions for the final time. I could see past the wind farms glinting in the distance to the rusted sea forts, the horizon's rotten teeth. Staring back out at the ocean, there was a moment when it almost seemed too clear a view, as though the unresolvedness of Caroline's mystery meant a thick fog should roll in on the wind. Like me, Dee, Beth, Ruby and some of the other neighbours had invested a great deal of time and energy in trying to find out who Caroline was and why she had walked out of this building. It was no small undertaking. On many occasions they'd shared what they'd learnt with me, so it felt right that I break this next bit of news face to face.

I would have liked to have been able to tell them that Caroline changed her mind. That I'd turned up on her doorstep one morning and made a heartfelt plea for her to reconsider so powerful she was moved to tell me her story: this is who I was, this is who I am. But that is not what happened. It is nothing more than another fantasy about Caroline Lane, every bit as speculative as my imagined iterations of her fate. In reality, we wouldn't be getting the answers we sought or anything close to them. Once again, Caroline would be characterised by what wasn't there rather than what was.

It must be said, though, that my motivations for going to Saltwater Mansions were less courteous than they were selfish. I thought that if I could share my lack of catharsis with others, it might diminish its potency somehow. I might finally be able to move on.

The atmosphere in the building was strange. It was a few degrees colder than it normally seemed, and a young couple I'd not seen before were speaking in hushed tones at the foot of the stairwell. Beth came to meet me at the entrance to her flat. Before she invited me in she checked the corridor for signs of her neighbours, as though she didn't want to be spotted or drawn into conversation. It was clear something was troubling her. As soon as I was sure we wouldn't be overheard, I asked her what it was. 'The fucking fire escape,' she said with a snarl.

At a recent meeting of the management company, the residents of Saltwater Mansions learnt that one of Mrs Bennett's dog's paws had almost fallen through a hole that had opened up on the networks of landings and steps at the back of the building. Metalwork experts had since inspected the structure and found it to be in imminent danger of collapse. They immediately had it condemned by the council, who gave strict orders: it needed to be replaced, and it needed to happen quickly. Not for the first time, the sums quoted for this job drew gasps, then silenced the room.

Some of the residents blamed their neighbours. Rumours were circulating that certain members of the management company – people who should know better – were still going up and down the outside stairs to their flats every day, even though the fire escape had been taped off and it might actually kill them and anyone unlucky enough to be close by if it fell apart. Ultimately, though, it didn't really matter whom anyone held responsible. The leaseholders' contract they'd signed when they moved in meant they were all on the hook. Every single homeowner would be responsible for a percentage of the overall cost proportional to their living space. Beth was slowly beginning to realise that her days of management company-related woe were not behind her after all. Because her flat was on the ground floor, she would owe a huge sum of money despite the fact that the fire escape was something she'd never need to use. This might not have been Caroline's living room any more, but she was in Caroline's shoes.

'What do you mean Caroline won't talk to you?' Dee said when I told her the news. 'Why would she not talk to you?' Her reaction was not dissimilar to my own. When I received Meredith's email ending our short dialogue, my surprise rapidly became indignation too. An answer to the question of who Caroline was had felt as though it was finally within my grasp. Now it was being denied. I'd been complaining about it to anyone who'd listen for weeks.

It was an ugly thing to admit, but there was a level on which I felt that I was owed an explanation about Caroline. Particularly after all the time and effort it had taken to reach this point; I'd been the one to let her know all of her possessions had been sold, donated or destroyed. But, as frustrating and disappointing as the Lane family's *omertà* might have been, I could see that my feeling aggrieved was an entitled and unreasonable response. Not that it mattered. It didn't stop me feeling it. If anything frustrated and disappointed me, perhaps it should have been that. The simple fact of the matter was that her story was no more mine to tell than it had been mine to hear. No amount of striving to understand why she wouldn't talk would change such things, because why she wouldn't talk would remain as much of a mystery as the woman herself.

A part of me wondered what Meredith made of it all. After spending so long convinced that Caroline had nobody who missed her, I remained glad there was somebody out there providing the familial closeness I always feared she lacked. The many fates I'd imagined for Caroline might have been speculative or wide of the mark, but in every last one of them she would have benefited from having someone who loved her. I took comfort in the fact that Meredith was there for Caroline, to remember her, to care for her and to protect her.

Protection seemed to me to be the subtext of her final email; like it was something Caroline needed very much – why else would Meredith have made a point of saying she was a 'nice person'? Maybe the need for protection was why she left Saltwater Mansions in the first place. Maybe Meredith was frustrated by Caroline too. Whatever the situation, if Meredith hadn't known that her sister had a life in Margate, in some way Caroline Lane would always be a fiction. She would always be a story without an end. There would always be someone wanting to know it.

'So what are we meant to do now?' Beth said. The dog followed her around the room and moped as though it shared her befuddlement. I had no useful answer. It was hard not to imagine that, after all this time and focus, not getting to know who Caroline Lane truly was would stay with me. That I would always be aware of the absence of her story, and that this would be a source of pain that might dull but never really go away. Looking back, I can see that here I am describing a feeling akin to the loss of a loved one. And that makes perfect sense to me now. What is grief if not the pain of absence? A life is a story after all.

I said goodbye to Dee and Beth and stepped out of Saltwater Mansions. It was midday and a low-slung sun lit the ocean. As I walked towards the station, I thought of how, if Caroline had taken the train out of Margate that day, with no bag on her shoulder and no wish to return, this is the way she'd have gone. Along the coast. Up the promenade. Through a town as it teetered once more on the cusp of change.

A little further down the road I cut through to the spindly streets of Cliftonville. Here I saw a team of builders dragging a shop's rotted wooden innards on to the pavement. A man approached, carrying a plastic bag full of cans that swung like udders. He asked what they were turning it into; it was an off-licence until as recently as a couple of months ago, where he bought beer and tobacco. He liked the man who owned it – they used to swap gossip about all the goings on in the neighbourhood – and hadn't seen him for a while. The builders told him they didn't know about the man, but it'd be an art gallery soon. 'Great,' he said, 'another one. Just what we fucking need.'

As I continued onwards I saw that the faded signs of old stores were being replaced with the shiny, hand-drawn liveries of new businesses so quickly it was a struggle to remember what was there before: whether the pizza parlour was where the pound shop used to be, if the sushi place was a mobility scooter dealership, or the wine bar where you could get a loan secured on a Christening bracelet when times got especially tough.

The crumbled ruins of an old guest house had been turned into a chic hotel by wealthy investors who, in the final stages of gentrification, could smell money coming somewhere down the line. The yard that sold art made on scrap and old bits of fairground junk had been swallowed by overpriced apartments. Gone was the man who'd offer you a substantial cash reward for information on 'the cockroach' that ordered a hit on his son.

The scuffs were being painted over, the creases ironed flat, the edges smoothed, the outsiders forced out, their stories all fading from view. A cultural homogeneousness prevailed; the colours were all the same hue. As I walked down through the Old Town, across the cobbled road towards the ocean, I couldn't help but think that, if what you wanted to find was a mystery around here, it might get harder and harder to know where to look.

Sitting on the steps at the base of the harbour arm, I watched the tide edge out like someone trying not to wake a sleeping lover. I've always associated the sea with an ending. I hadn't realised it at the time, but in all four of the books I've written before, the story ends at the sea on the final page. If it bore light analysis, I might say it's because, on some subconscious level, when you reach the sea your journey is complete. There is nowhere else to go.

This didn't feel like an ending to me.

Over time – because in the intense opacity of feeling, grief conceals itself from you until the things it makes you do, the things you need to do to keep going, are done – I would come to see what had been hidden from me all along. It would all begin to make enough sense for me to finally be able to start letting go of Caroline Lane. If I didn't feel like the story ended here, it was because Caroline's story was not the one I'd been telling. It's a different story entirely, the story that ends by the sea.

I've often found that, when your focus is consumed by a thing and it's all you think and feel and talk about, you start to see that thing reflected in the world around you. If you were studying butterflies, you might start to see more butterflies fluttering around the flowers in your garden. You might spot them popping up in books you're reading, or flitting past in the background of a television show. You might overhear someone talking about butterflies in a cafe, or notice the shape of one in the pattern on a friend's wallpaper. It can be the same with extremes of emotion. If we break up with someone we love, suddenly everyone is holding hands. If a dog dies, we see dogs everywhere. If we bury a sibling, everybody else has a brother. It'll seem as though love and grief attract echoes like a table might dust.

It is not that our fixations are magnetic, or that the universe mirrors the river of our thinking. But by having these experiences and thinking these thoughts; by pursuing, by suffering or obsessing over them, we make ourselves alive to their presence in the world. They are there no more than normal, but we notice them now. They play at a frequency that suddenly we hear, precisely because we need to hear it.

So it was that, around the time I received Meredith's final email, I started to hear about people vanishing without resolution; without their stories ever being known. In one, a man was found wandering the seafront in Dorset. He was roughly fifty years old and slim, with long, matted hair and a brown beard, and could not tell the police his name, where he'd come from, or for how long he'd been walking. In another, a lady's body was found in a London flat, unnoticed by anyone for almost three years. Unmissed, it would seem, by everyone she had ever met.

And then, one day, a woman in Lancashire went for a walk.

The banks of the Wyre were frozen. They were thick with mud and strewn with leaves. But Dan Duffy was undeterred. Any spare time he had he spent searching the pathways by the river. Even by night he'd be there. Rummaging through bushes. Peering into shadows. Following leads and tip-offs on suspicious activity, like men burning rubbish, or lights in an abandoned house. Whatever it was, he'd investigate. He wanted answers. How can it be that an ordinary woman goes missing like that? How does someone simply vanish without trace? It didn't make sense to Dan at all. In fact, it stank. He was sure there was something more to it. Something bigger. That he was only ever a moment away from finding what he so desperately sought.

He wasn't alone. There were thousands of people watching the footage he live-streamed from his phone as he went about his investigations. The more he searched, the more they encouraged him. They told him he was doing a good job and that it was important work. They said he shouldn't be put off by the locals any more than he should let the police throw him off the scent; that meant he was getting closer to the truth. He was a hero. That's what they said, and they said it over and over. It was nice to be admired. It felt good to be of use.

Three weeks earlier was the last ordinary morning in St Michael's on Wyre. Nicola Bulley was working through a familiar routine. She got up. Had breakfast. Dropped the kids off at school. It was still early, cold out. She took her springer spaniel for a walk by the river. The dog's name was Willow, a bouncy, lively thing.

She sent a text to a friend arranging a playdate for her daughter later in the week, then logged into a work call on Microsoft Teams. Nicola was a mortgage broker and these things could go on for ages. Online meetings were something she was used to. The novelty of them in the early days of lockdown had passed. Back then, people did their make-up and straightened the living room. Now everyone was more relaxed. It wasn't unusual for her microphone to be muted, or for her to be walking the dog while they talked. For nobody to be able to see or hear what happened next.

Nicola's phone was discovered on a bench half an hour later, still connected to the call. Willow was found alone close by, her harness in the mud by the water.

Not only could Lancashire Constabulary find no sign of Nicola, they found no sign of suspicious activity, criminal behaviour or third-party involvement either. There was no CCTV footage. No dash-cams caught Nicola leaving the area, or anyone unusual entering it. Their working hypothesis was that this was a tragic accident. That she'd fallen into the Wyre. The water was fast-flowing and cold, so it was easy to see how falling in might be lethal. But repeated searches of the bank and the river all the way down to the sea found nothing.

Nicola's partner Paul told a journalist he was unconvinced. She can't have gone into the water. His beliefs were substantiated when an independent team of specialists searched the river using side-scan sonar and concluded their operation without finding anything. Not even an item of clothing. The team's leader, Peter Faulding, a world-renowned confined space rescue and forensic search expert, said that in his entire twenty-year career he'd never seen anything so unusual as this.

St Michael's on Wyre suddenly found itself besieged by the media. The villagers couldn't drive their cars through the square for satellite vans. They couldn't leave their houses without a reporter pointing a camera in their direction, asking what they thought had happened, where Nicola might have been, what else they knew about the woman who'd vanished. How were they supposed to respond to questions that had no answers?

The poor family, the bereft friends, the stony-faced police

and hard-working search teams, the clamorous media and the bewildered residents – these were all people you'd expect to find on the scene of a high-profile disappearance. That's how they tend to go. But there was another group of people in St Michael's on Wyre that day and on the long, dark days that followed. An unexpected group none of the others had really encountered before. Not on a scene like this.

They looked like ordinary folk. They were wearing big coats and woolly hats and drinking Costa coffee from red paper cups. But they weren't concerned locals. They'd come from all over. And they weren't just meandering around the village and then moving on either, rubber-necking like people do when something terrible happens and worst instincts kick in. No, they were gathering near the bench where Nicola Bulley's dog and phone were found, where the dive teams were searching the water, to keep an eye on proceedings. To trade theories. To figure things out. To do their bit. They thought of themselves not as shocked bystanders, but as citizen journalists-cum-detectives, looking for a truth they were sure was being hidden from view.

One reporter, Darryl Morris from Times Radio, grew tired of waiting for police updates and turned his attention to the people by the bench. He asked a woman what she was doing hanging out at the place where a missing person was last seen. She explained that she was from nearby Preston.

'[I just want to] have a look, have a walk round,' she said. 'It's so close to home, I've got kids myself. Just wanna do our bit . . . come and help. Be other sets of eyes.' Morris suggested that some people might think the woman and her friends could be a hindrance to the official investigation, no matter how good their intentions. This was a sensitive matter. Time was of the essence. Preserving the location was key.

Crowds of people gathering around the place might make that more difficult than it needed to be. The woman was unmoved.

'We've all got eyes,' she said, 'we can all look.' The way she saw it, they weren't so different from the detectives. It didn't matter whether they had a badge or not, they all wanted the same thing: Nicola Bulley found. But there was a sense among them that they were bringing something to the table the detectives with badges couldn't. Unlike the police, who had quotas, scrutiny and the force's self-preservation to worry about, they didn't have agendas beyond their concern for Nicola Bulley's welfare. They might look at it from a fresh perspective. Plus, like Nicola Bulley, they were mothers. They felt an emotional connection to the story that a lumbering old institution prone to malfeasance like the police couldn't hope to replicate.

Morris told the woman that some members of the press had labelled them 'grief junkies'. She pointed to the journalists clustered on the riverbank and fired back. They might consider themselves trained, regulated professionals covering a public-interest story. They might say they're holding the police to account. But they were still here because a woman had gone missing. They were still using an emotive tragedy to create content used to sell newspapers or television advertising space. Were they not grief junkies too?

Dan Duffy was also there that day. In the background, hanging around. Some of the press had seen him before. He was a regular. They thought him a bit of a nuisance, in fact.

'It would be nice to discover this lady,' he told Morris. 'Be the guy known as the hero. And that's what I'm trying to do. A hero sort of thing. Like, wow, someone's actually found her. If someone has got her captive or something like that. Just like a hero. A real-life superhero.'

Duffy had been chronicling his efforts to find Nicola Bulley on YouTube over the last few days. He'd made long videos of himself patrolling the village with a torch, talking about how there were lots of theories going around on the internet, and how he was just trying to get to the truth. In one video he gets excited as he looks beneath an abandoned sheet of tarpaulin. In another he finds a soft piece of ground underfoot, and says it feels like 'someone's covered something up. Look at this! It does feel soft here. Like it's been freshly dug!'

While Duffy was wrong about the tarpaulin and the soft ground, he was right about the internet. Nicola Bulley's case had given rise to a troubling industry of online gossip. Rumours about her home life, relationship, finances and mental state were going viral. Strangers shared documents they claimed showed she was going bust. Had she faked her own death? Had she been killed by her partner? Was it an insurance job? The clamour for 'truth', which a lot of people now thought at odds with the version of the truth put out through official channels they could no longer trust, was in some ways becoming a bigger story than the story itself.

Events were metastasising in a way that quickly threatened to make the search untenable. And, for the villagers of St Michael's on Wyre, frightening. There were strangers all over the place looking for clues. Some of the residents employed an external security company to keep amateur investigators off their property. Wyre Council leader Michael Vincent said: 'People have reported being sat in their living rooms in an afternoon watching television, and people coming up to the windows, peering in, trying the doors. It's been terrifying for them. These are typically older people extremely scared in their own homes.'

On 15 February, Lancashire Constabulary held a press conference. Assistant Chief Constable Peter Lawson and Detective Superintendent Rebecca Smith told a room full of journalists that there remained no evidence of criminal activity or third-party involvement in Nicola Bulley's disappearance. In effect, there was no news to report. Instead, they'd gathered to acknowledge the fact that their relative silence on developments in the case had fed the clamour to hunt and share them online.

The police decided to attack this on two fronts. The first made sense. They wanted to discourage people from speculating on social media and, worse still, those 'playing private detective' who were now turning up around the Wyre in droves. The two things combined were creating a flood of false information and mawkish rumour that had been detrimental to the police investigation and adversely affected Nicola Bulley's family. As a result, the police were putting in place a dispersal order to prevent any further disruption. If you were a nuisance, you'd be moved on.

The second was more ham-fisted. In what seemed like an attempt to debunk the armchair sleuths and internet speculators' criticisms of the investigation and wild murder theories, the police released information which, by dint of the fact it was being released at all, would have the very opposite effect. They told the press that Nicola Bulley had specific vulnerabilities relating to alcohol and the menopause. It was a strange level of detail to divulge, certainly not the kind of thing normally shared in an active missing person's investigation. It was a contravention of their duty to the Bulley family's care, and a sexist act that both discredited her and provided grist to the mill for anyone who still suspected all was not quite what it seemed.

Dan Duffy was one of them. He remained convinced that

Nicola's disappearance involved foul play, and that he might be the one to crack it. Even though he'd already been there a few times and had been warned to stay clear, he was sure there was more to the abandoned house a few fields away than the police were letting on. He'd heard people had been spotted up there. That they'd seen lights and movement inside. By now there was barely an inch of St Michael's on Wyre he hadn't examined as part of his investigation. The abandoned house really stuck out. It was remote. Big. Difficult to access. What better place to hold someone hostage – or hide a body – than that?

But on his next trip there was a confrontation. One of the villagers had grown sick of what the amateur sleuths were doing to the area. The way they went stomping around late at night, looking into people's private property. He confronted Duffy and told him to desist. Duffy warned the man not to put his hands on him, even though he hadn't. He said the man might regret it if he did. It felt like there might be violence, a repellent urgency in the air.

The livestream went bananas. Why would Duffy – a good, honourable, brave man – be meeting such resistance from the villagers if he wasn't on to something? The people watching at home, tens of thousands of them by now, told Dan that he had to keep searching. They said that the men trying to prevent him from wandering the streets around their houses late at night had 'shady faces'. One said those stopping him now looked like suspects.

The next video to appear on Duffy's YouTube channel was of his arrest. It's early in the morning. He's wearing a large black vest. His eyes are sleepy and his hair is flat; he looks like he's been yanked out of bed. He's being handcuffed by officers in his home, peering into his own camera, saying: 'Hey guys, I'm being arrested on a public-order offence. They've had an allegation. As you all know I was in a search to find the missing woman Nicola, but this is what this country's turning into. No freedom of speech.'

A statement released later by the police confirmed that a 36-year-old man from Darwen, Lancashire was arrested under Section Four of the Public Order Act for Fear/Provocation of Violence. He was given a fixed penalty notice of £90. TikTok subsequently removed Duffy's videos for multiple violations, saying they did not tolerate bullying or harassment on their platform, and removed content that violated their policies. The video of his arrest was his most-watched yet.

Four days later, on 19 February, a man and a woman were out walking their dog about a mile downstream of St Michael's on Wyre when they noticed something unusual in the water. Police set up a tent on the bank and a helicopter hovered above as Nicola Bulley's body was recovered from the reeds. Across on the far bank a man was arrested after climbing over a fence, passing through a police cordon and trying to film the body. When questioned, he told police he was a journalist.

Nicola was identified by her dental records. The following June, an inquest would hear that her Fitbit suggested she entered the water at 9.22. The cause of her death was established to be drowning. There was no evidence she had been harmed before she went into the river that day. There was no reason to believe it was anything more than a terrible accident.

After Nicola Bulley was found, the grief tourists started to disperse. The police and the journalists and the villagers were quietly keen never to see the likes of them again. But they privately suspected that the next time someone went missing and the story blew up to become a high-profile case, people just like them would be there.

They thought the grief junkies' motivations were misguided. That they'd been warped by the boom in internet conspiracy theories foisted on them by an algorithm that monetised the suspicions it stoked. Bent by overexposure to true-crime podcasts, books, magazines, TV dramas and documentaries. Shaped by a prevailing air of public distrust in the establishment that made them feel overlooked and underserved, unheard and lied to, they'd come and stand out in the cold, day after day, just to look out for one of their own, down by the churn of the Wyre.

And maybe all of that was true. But none of the reporters took the time to try and get to know any of them like Darryl Morris did. That was how he'd spent most of his days while he waited for developments in the search. Just chatting to them, asking them about their stories. They all had one, if you drilled deep enough.

There was one man who was there almost every day, standing near the bench with his red paper cup, peering down at the water. He'd lost four of his grandchildren in a house fire ten years previously. That's why he came here really, he said. He'd heard about the missing woman and it chimed with the pain inside him. Made the pain feel like it was reaching out and searching for something that felt as hollow as itself. He just wanted to find Nicola. And to see the family. To show them that they, and he, weren't alone.

And Dan Duffy. Dan Duffy's sister died in 2011. No one knows how. There's an open verdict. It's a mystery. He thinks about her all the time. It's never really stopped, the pain. It's always there, always on. How do you make it go away? Loss is drawn to loss. Grief is drawn to grief. When you can't find the answers to the questions in your heart you'll search anywhere.

Fifteen

There were stories my family returned to, fixed points where we could find each other, buoys in the ocean of our past. My favourite was the one about Mum and Dad going shopping and running into Dad's cousin. Dad asked her how her mother was and she reminded him he'd been at her funeral a couple of years before. Like his refusal to talk about himself, his bad timing became something else we thought about when we thought about him. We always said it was a knack. It was an affliction.

On the day Mum told me Dad had cancer there was a story on the front page of the newspaper warning that the pandemic was especially terrible news for cancer patients. The disease had taken advantage of his gift for bad timing. While he'd been on the phone to doctors he couldn't see face to face for months, getting prescribed five courses of antibiotics for an infection that had never existed, the cancer marauded through his lower body, ransacking his bladder, prostate and lymph nodes. Now the oncologist spoke of a stark choice. Dad could have immediate, radical, life-changing surgery, or he could die. Dad told them to cut him open and get the cancer out. To do it on the floor of the office right now, if they had the tools. I consoled myself by clinging to his bloody-minded gift for getting shit done. He wanted to live, so he would. I cried in the park that day. There were no planes. It felt like a slight that the sky should stay so untroubled.

The first time Dad and I spoke after the operation his voice sounded different. It had always been deep and growly. Now there was less bass in it. Less gravel. I asked if they'd removed so many of his internal organs that the acoustics inside his body had changed, like seats ripped out of the Royal Albert Hall. He thought I was imagining things. That his voice only sounded weak because he was tired. All he needed was rest and soon enough he'd be back on his feet.

Dad's car wasn't anything special, but he loved that car and he fixated on the day he got to drive it again. If he was able to drive, the phone could be switched back on and people could call on him to do things for them and everything would be as it was before he got sick. There was a long way to go. First he had to stand up. Then get used to walking in tiny steps. To build his strength and stamina from nothing to something again. But he was determined. His glacial, months-long journey from armchair to car became an unofficial barometer of his recovery. The further he got, the better he was.

Covid meant we weren't allowed to visit in case we killed him, so Mum would update us on his progress. I liked hearing how he'd reached the far end of the room, then the window, then the door. On the day months later when she called to say she'd caught him sitting in the driver's seat, singing along to ABBA's 'The Winner Takes It All', we finally allowed ourselves to believe what he'd never shown himself to doubt. That he would be OK. A song about the cruelty of divorce, repurposed as an ode to the ecstasy of survival.

When I was young I played on the corner of our street with my brother and his friends most evenings. We kicked a ball around, and if it went over somebody's fence we'd have to climb into their garden to retrieve it, hoping we wouldn't be caught. Sometimes we went home when we were hungry, but usually we waited until it was dark.

It was dark that evening when the ambulance came and stopped outside our house. The night sky flashed a looping blue. We raced back as quickly as we could. A team of paramedics were urgently unfolding a bed on the pavement. We were intercepted by our neighbours. They took us into their lounge and fed us biscuits. There was no limit to the amount we were allowed to eat because my granddad had died on the bathroom floor of our house next door just a half hour or so before.

On the night of the funeral Dad took me to the park on my bike. I looped around the track a few times and then we sat on the grass. He asked me to pick out the brightest star in the sky. It was obvious. One of them was more brilliant, its light so much whiter and more urgent than the others. I pointed to it and he said that one was granddad. It struck me as being a poetic thing to say. I'd never really heard him say anything like that before. I didn't after, either. We looked up at it for a while. I looked at him but he was still looking up. He didn't want me to see his eyes.

Thirty years passed before I thought of that night again. I was holding my own son then. He was a few hours old, his flesh soft as virgin dough. I'd expected my love for him to be complex in some way. It wasn't. My love for him was big and simple – I was his father and he was my son – but it still felt impossible to communicate. I wondered if I'd ever be able to describe it to him. How do you describe a world?

When I told Dad that I named my son Douglas, after his father, after my grandfather, he looked up at the stars.

Mum said Dad would look small when we visited him in the hospital. It felt like she'd made a mistake. Dad wasn't small. He was broad and strong. But then everything about his cancer felt like a mistake. Dad was the wrong person. The surgeon should have been able to get it all. The immunotherapy should have worked. Dad should never have confused it with aromatherapy in a meeting with one of Britain's top oncologists. The cancer should never have spread into his lungs, but it did, hiding there as death should.

I spent the few days before thinking of what I might say when I first got there. I wanted it to be something funny to make him forget about cancer, so I told him I'd crashed his car. He said it wouldn't matter if I had. What matters is we're all OK. He had the same smile from their wedding photograph. Fifty years ago. Mum in her dress. Dad in his uniform. All that love, it leads you here. Small somehow but still handsome, being held.

A consultant came to update him on how the chemotherapy was going. He was younger than it seemed an expert should be, with warm brown eyes. He sat on the bed and pulled his mask down over his chin. There were laughter lines round his mouth. His face was kind, or I wanted it to be.

'Hello Mr Whitehouse,' he said. 'How are you feeling?'

'Not bad,' Dad said.

The doctor nodded. He held Dad's hand. Dad looked at him and smiled. He told Dad he had six weeks to live and Dad said OK as though it was OK. The doctor said sorry and left and Mum was crying. I told Dad I was sorry. He asked what for. I told him I was sorry that everything was so terrible for him. 'Don't worry about that,' he said. What he meant was he didn't want to talk about himself.

When he came home four days later they unloaded him from the ambulance and he seemed annoyed to find us waiting on the pavement. He asked what we were all doing, standing there, mad that we would get cold over something so inconsequential as his return. I thought about how this would be the last time he'd enter through his own front door. How it was all lasts from here on in. His skin clung to his bones like wet silk.

The front room was a makeshift hospital room now. We helped him on to the bed. He was light, his arm round my neck, thin and weak like a boy's. The journey from the hospital had exhausted him. He needed to rest. I asked him if he wanted to sleep and he said yes, in a minute. He asked me how my children were. I told him they were fine. I wanted to tell him that they loved him, but it seemed too final. Not yet. There was still time. We had six weeks for that. Go to sleep, I said. I'll see you in a while. When he was asleep I said I love you. I hadn't said that to him since I was a child. I'd waited until he was asleep.

Death stirs the experience of others. In their eyes the embers left by grief glow bright again a little. They say that you should make sure you have all the conversations you want to have, ask all the questions you want to ask, say all the things you want to say. It was presumptuous to assume that Dad might want to spend the last six weeks of his life talking about himself when he'd spent the previous seventy-two years avoiding it. The idea that death would be the spur he'd need to tell me his story was a fantasy I'd concocted to lose myself in, rather than confront what was soon coming. But when I packed my bag to move back into my parents' house with my brother and sister – this little house we all grew up in, where we would be until the end – I packed my old dictaphone, just in case. We had six weeks, after all.

That was what I wanted to do. I would ask him everything I should have asked him before, and he would tell me anything he wanted to tell me. There would be nothing left unsaid. I'd know his story. I'd know who he was then and always would. It would be known.

We knew but never knew we were running out of time. Dad did not wake up.

While Grace cut my hair we made small talk about how hot it was outside and compared notes on our children's teachers. She wanted to know about my latest book, so we spoke for a while about that, and she asked what I was working on next. The truth was nothing, but I didn't feel able to get into the reasons why, so instead I said I didn't really know. The real answer was that I hadn't been doing any work recently. The two weeks since my father died had been lost to a grief thick as smoke. This was why I came to her salon in the first place, to get my hair cut for the funeral. But I didn't want to burden her with my pain, even though I was sure she could see it moving the air around me.

There was a pause then, a brief moment of silence that at the time felt natural, but which, on reflection, Grace might have manufactured, as if to bring my focus to what she was about to say, this thing that I might need to hear.

'I've got a story for you,' she said. It was something her previous client, Dee, whose hair Grace dyed pale pink, had told her just an hour or so before. 'I haven't been able to stop thinking about it since. I'll tell you. But if I do, you won't be able to stop thinking about it either.' The scissors were still and her eyes were vivid. This was her guarantee.

Between Grace's salon and Saltwater Mansions was the harbour arm, a stone pier that stretched out into the sea, draped round the shoulders of the town, shielding it from the violence in the water. Sometimes, when I was out walking and thinking about Caroline Lane, this is where I'd find myself. Before you reach the lighthouse there's a small pub. Plastic crabs hang from the ceiling. You can buy a beer, drink it on the roof and watch the pyrotechnics of a Margate sundown. Ocean foam floats on the breeze and lips sting in salt air. The waves come and they come. I found it comforting to know this happened yesterday and would happen tomorrow, whether we're here or not.

Dad once sat on this roof with my children in his arms. Some collusion of the gruffness in his voice and the way he magicked chocolate from behind their ears inspired a love in them that was closer to awe. They jiggled in his lap and laughed when he chased them along the harbour wall.

In the hours before he died I sat in his old leather armchair and watched him sleep. A soft dawn light seeped through the curtains and played upon his cheekbones. I took a photo of his fading tattoos. His breathing slowed to a gentle rasp, the hummingbird snore of a child. We knew one another. I held his hand.

Dad's funeral took place in a crematorium on the hottest day on record. It was a fitting final act for a man with bad timing. People stood in rows three deep at the back. I'd never met most of them before and they'd never met each other, but Dad did their shopping, drove them to their hospital appointments, changed their lightbulbs and fixed their toasters. He picked them up and dropped them off. He checked in on them and went out for them. He kept them company when they were lonely. He did what they needed whenever they asked. All they had to do was call.

My sister, brother and I took it in turns to stand at the front and talk about our father's life. It was impossible to do, but we did it. We told them he was the boy who holidayed on the beach. He was the teenager who sailed the ocean. He was the sailor who married the woman he loved. He was the father who picked up his kids when they were lost. He was the granddad holding two children at sunset. He was a man who did things for people. That was his story. It was told.

We put his ashes in a little cardboard boat and pushed it out into the sea.

Sources

p.6 – 'This Little Wiggy', *The Simpsons* (S9.E19), 22 March 1998.

pp.182–3; 188 – All quotes from Darryl Morris are from the following sources:

The Story: Stories of Our Times podcast by *The Times*. 'Nicola Bulley and the TikTok detectives', Manveen Rana and Darryl Morris, 17 February 2023. Available at: https://shows.acast.com/storiesofourtimes/episodes/nicola-bulley-and-the-tiktok-detectives

Darryl Morris. 'Searching for Nicola: TikTok Sleuths and "Grief Junkies"', Darrylmorris.co.uk, February 2023. Available at: https://darrylmorris.co.uk/2023/02/15/searching-for-nicola-tiktok-sleuths-and-grief-junkies/

For the sections about Margate's transformation, I repeatedly returned to the book *Gentrification Is Inevitable and Other Lies* by Leslie Kern (Verso, 2022).

Acknowledgements

I am fortunate that, when I fell down the rabbit hole of Caroline Lane, some brilliant and clear-eyed people came with me. Without the talent, insight and patience of my editor Francesca Main, I would not have been able to write this book. If it wasn't for her stewardship, sensitivity and belief, I might still be falling. I am grateful that we get to work together, and consider myself lucky that this collaboration and friendship goes on.

When I told my friend Rachel Boot about Caroline, an obsession was shared. Her enthusiasm propelled the writing of this book through the tricky early stages. I am thankful for the endless Caroline conversations, theory swapping, recording help and willingness to go with me, pulling threads. Neither of us guessed how it might go.

Dee, Leonard, Beth, Grace and all those who shared their stories with me for this book were deeply generous with their time and truth, and my gratitude is due to them. As it is to my agent, Cathryn Summerhayes, who is always there with advice and encouragement. Thank you, Cath.

I'd also like to give thanks to the world-beating teams at Phoenix and Orion, Alice Graham, Tom Noble, Katie Espiner, Aoife Datta, Susie Bertinshaw and many more. Their support means a great deal to me. The same goes for Amanda

Davis, Max Grant, Doireann Cooke and Annabel White at Curtis Brown.

Writing this book was difficult at times. Talking to or moaning at some fantastic writers helped. Thank you to Michael Holden and Harriet Gibsone for listening.

The love and kindness of my family makes things possible. Lou, Douglas and Elmer, I love you. Love and thanks too to Mum (at the time of writing it is bright and the water is calm, down at Minehead harbour), Alison, Glenn, Darren, Alex, William, Oliver, Thomas, Anna, Jonathan and the Jakemans.

Credits

Phoenix Books and David Whitehouse would like to thank everyone at Orion who worked on the publication of *Saltwater Mansions*.

Agent
Cathryn Summerhayes, Curtis Brown

Editor
Francesca Main

Copy-editor
Linden Lawson

Proofreader
Laetitia Grant

Editorial Management
Susie Bertinshaw
Alice Graham
Jane Hughes
Charlie Panayiotou
Lucy Bilton
Patrice Nelson

Audio
Paul Stark
Louise Richardson
Georgina Cutler-Ross

Contracts
Rachel Monte
Ellie Bowker
Tabitha Gresty

Design
Charlotte Abrams-Simpson
Nick Shah
Deborah Francois
Helen Ewing
Steve Marking
Loveday May

Photo Shoots & Image Research
Natalie Dawkins

Finance
Nick Gibson
Jasdip Nandra
Sue Baker
Tom Costello

Inventory
Jo Jacobs
Dan Stevens

Production
Hannah Cox
Katie Horrocks

Marketing
Tom Noble

Publicity
Aoife Datta

Sales
Dave Murphy
Victoria Laws
Esther Waters
Group Sales teams across Digital, Field, International and Non-Trade

Operations
Group Sales Operations team

Rights
Tara Hiatt
Marie Henckel

'I feel very lucky to have read this book. Extraordinary and important . . . a triumph'
Adam Kay

'I was utterly floored by the emotional depth of *About A Son* – a book that reaches so deeply into the human experience that to read it is to be forever changed'
Elizabeth Day

One night in October 2015, twenty-year-old Morgan Hehir went out with friends and never came home.

In the aftermath of his funny, talented son's murder, Morgan's father Colin began to keep an extraordinary diary. It became a record of his family's grief, the ensuing trial, and his determined quest to uncover the shocking truth that the police had kept hidden.

Inspired by this diary, About A Son *is a groundbreaking work of creative non-fiction that asks vital questions about the nature of justice and pays tribute to the unbreakable bond between a father and son.*

Read on for an extract from *About A Son*, available now in paperback, ebook and audio

There's a fountain in the centre of town. Every summer, bored teenagers uphold a mischievous tradition to fill it with bubble bath. The falling water churns the soap until the foam outswells the fountain's walls and blows through the streets on the breeze. It floats past bemused shoppers, angry market traders and delighted children, who imagine themselves tumbling, as though the whole of Nuneaton is inside the spinning silver drum of a giant washing machine. That it will come out sparkly and new. They're too young to see that which can't be cleaned, the dirt around the edges of a place like this. The stains left on the fabric of a town by its tragedies.

On the evening of 31 October 2015, near the outskirts of Nuneaton town centre less than half a mile from here, twenty-year-old Morgan Hehir was walking through a park with five friends when they were viciously attacked by three strangers. One of them had a knife. Morgan was stabbed to death.

The brutality and senselessness of Morgan's murder shocked the town. It was impossible to live there, or have lived there, and not hear about it. It was impossible not to feel it in your bones when you did.

Though I left Nuneaton in 1999, when I was eighteen, Morgan's life had been lived and taken on the streets of my formative years. He'd worked at the hospital where I was born, and where my mother worked until her retirement. He'd spray-painted graffiti in the park where I misspent my adolescence. He'd been walking between two pubs where I had some of my first underage drinks when he was murdered by a young man who'd once done the same. We never knew one another, Morgan and I, but I'd been him in the past.

I followed the story from afar, through tired eyes on a phone screen late at night as I fed my baby son. Old school friends discussed new developments on Facebook. Some knew of the young man who lost his life, others the people who took it. My mother would mention his name when we spoke.

'How could they do something so wicked?' she would say, about the killers. It was a question to which no answer ever came.

A little over four years after Morgan's death, in January 2020, I received an email from Claire Harrison, a reporter on the *Nuneaton News*. I'd been friends with Claire since primary school; we were fixtures at each other's childhood birthday parties. She had covered Morgan's murder, the trial of his killers, and his father Colin Hehir's tireless search for the truth about the individual and systemic failures that led to his son's death. As a result, she'd become friends with Colin, who had recently sent her an extraordinary document.

The day after finding out Morgan had been murdered, and motivated only by the desire not to forget a single detail of the ordeal he and his family were about to endure, Colin experienced a remarkable moment of clarity in the thick fog of sorrow. He began to take notes. He'd never written anything longer than a shopping list before, but now he had 164 pages amounting to a diary of events that, in the opening paragraph, promised to 'tell you about the shit we have been through . . . tell the story of what happened'.

Colin wanted Claire's opinion on what he should do with his diary. He wanted as many people to know Morgan's story as possible. Should he post it online? Self-publish it? Would anyone even be interested, or had he lost his mind? Claire wasn't sure. But she offered to send the document to me on the basis that I'd written some books, that I knew the town, and that I may have some ideas.

The truth was, I didn't. I'd never read anything like it before. Colin's diary was a unique record of grief, told from a place deep within it. Of what happens to a parent when a child is taken from them in such sudden, terrible and tragic circumstances. Of how a family picks up the broken pieces and puts itself back together, but only ever in the wrong shape. Of how ordinary people live lives made anything but ordinary by the explosive violence of a young man with a knife. Of how so many families suffer such senseless loss we never hear about. And of how the systems designed to protect us will contort to protect themselves when they fail.

It was a report from the front line of loss. Rough, angry, moving, tender, maddening and blindingly honest, a testament not just to his son's life, but Colin's refusal to give up until he discovered the truth of how Morgan's murder came to be – a murder that should never have taken place.

Though utterly compelling, Colin's diary was intensely personal, overwhelmingly raw and indescribably sad. It was sometimes difficult to read, sometimes impossible. What advice could I give to someone who'd known such pain about what to do with it? As a father of sons, what could I say to a man who had lost one? I wasn't even sure how to begin the conversation. And so, to my shame, I didn't have it. I put the file in a folder I told myself I'd return to, and promised

I'd call Colin when I knew what to say. But though his story didn't leave my mind, that day never arrived.

It was three months later, on 15 April 2020, when I received a message from Colin directly, politely and patiently asking for my gut feelings on what he called his ramblings. It was then that I read his diary again, and we began to talk. Slowly, a way of telling his family's story, in the hope it never happens to another, began to take shape.

That diary and those conversations became the backbone of this book, which also uses interviews, news articles, police reports, reportage and other materials to tell the story of his son, his family, and this time. I will always be honoured that Colin and his family – his wife Sue, and their sons Connor and Eamon – trusted me with his writings, with their experience, and with their pain. I hope only to have done justice to them, and to Morgan.